D0340734

W7-CFU-745

THE
GIFT
OF
PLAY

THE
GIFT
OF
PLAY

*And Why Young
Children Cannot Thrive
Without It*

Maria W. Piers
and
Genevieve Millet Landau

WALKER AND COMPANY ☀ NEW YORK

First published in the United States of America in 1980 by the Walker Publishing Company, Inc.

Published simultaneously in Canada by Beaverbooks, Limited, Don Mills, Ontario.

ISBN: 0-8027-0657-6

Library of Congress Catalog Card Number: 80-80455

Printed in the United States of America

Book design by Robert Barto

10   9   8   7   6   5   4   3   2   1

*To Irving B. Harris
in recognition of his caring
concern for children.*

Contents

The failure to value play... The biological role of play... First games... The life-saving powers of play... Play deprivation retards development... The importance of exploratory play... The into-everything toddler... How logical thought begins... The healing power of play... Turning the tables through play... Reliving painful experiences... Professional play therapy... Preparation for school... Play and problem solving... Language learning... The child's need for predictability

THE
GIFT
OF
PLAY

Introduction:
What Play Is
and What It Isn't

At the first National Conference on Play, which the authors of this book directed last year, we presented some of the findings of experts in child development on the vital role of play in learning, development and survival.

One of the educators attending our conference said to us afterward, "I still don't know what play is, but whatever it is, I like it." We feel the same way. Like that educator and the rest of the experts, we can't say precisely what play is. No one has yet formulated a definition of play, especially of child's play, which includes everything it is and leaves out everything it isn't. Perhaps this is because real child's play takes in so much of the child's world—indeed, virtually all of it—imbuing all of children's activities with a very special flavor.

In trying to define child's play, educators often say that play is the child's work. But this description, unfortunately, has led some parents and teachers to value only that play which seems to them to be really serious—play whose aim they recognize and approve of. In thinking of play as child's work, even those who appreciate its worth tend to value play principally to the extent that they can shape it and use it as a tool to teach young children the virtues of adult life—of hard work, persistence, prudence and ambition.

But this kind of adult-directed play rarely corresponds with real child's play. True child's play is largely self-motivated, self-designed, and often seems to the adult to have no serious aim at all.

We would rather think of the child's world of play not as the work-world of the adult, scaled down to child size, but as something more akin to a theatrical play. As the dramatist presents material intended to illuminate the lives of the audience, so does the child, the author of his play, illuminate the events of his inner and outer worlds. Child's play, like a theatrical play, symbolizes—is the key to understanding—the human condition.

Though we will not try to define play in a sentence or a paragraph in this book, we will try to describe the whole play universe of the young child and to show why it is the most important thing young children do—something they cannot do without.

CHAPTER
I

Lifeline to
Early Development

"I CAN'T see why we should send Jill to that nursery school. The kids don't learn anything there. All they do is play."

Plenty of parents and teachers consider child's play a luxury, merely a way of marking time between more important activities. The assumption that children at play are not learning anything valuable—not developing or being prepared for school and life—is distressingly widespread. It couldn't be more wrong.

Actually, there is a whole range of activities that are vitally important to children's development which we lump together under the word "play". And these play activities are the most important things young children do. Play is not merely the child's way of learning, it is the only good and lasting way of learning for the young child. Through play children learn and polish skills—social, emotional, physical, mental.

Even more, through imaginative play young children come to terms with many of the fears and hurts they're vulnerable to. They actually heal themselves of emotional injuries through play, coping with and mastering such common, potentially devastating occurrences as, for example, suffering a sudden separation from their parents. Without the chance to experience the natural healing power of imaginative play, the emotional wounds caused by such events might never close, leaving the child with a lifelong residue of anxiety and insecurity. If children did not play, they could not thrive, and they might not survive.

THE FAILURE TO
VALUE PLAY

Though play—self-motivated, discovery play—is vital to healthy development, many young children today are deprived of play opportunities, and worse, are actually being inhibited in their very capacity to play.

Some of the encroachments on young children's playtimes stem from the best of motives. Many parents and teachers are eager to provide preschool children with a sort of academic head start that will assure "success" in school. But they fail to understand what it is about play—and what play really is—that makes it, rather than specific school-readiness games and lessons, the surest, fastest path to learning, self-confidence and the mastery of many skills.

Some of the current limitations on children's opportunities to engage in imaginative play stem from the nature of contemporary society, from the lack of continuing connections between individual families and the rapidly changing world in which they live and work. Among these are the uprooted nature of contemporary life, with so many young parents living far from their families and the places where they grew up, and the impersonal kind of work so many parents go off to in the mornings and come home from in the evenings, bringing no real picture to their children of what their work is for, or what they really do.

These trends in family and social life deprive young children of the "raw material" they need for the let's-pretend-to-be games that are essential to their understanding of what the adult world is like and what they can do to find a good place in it for themselves.

Young children today are even further cut off from the real world—and from their inner selves—by a pervasive intruder in their lives that smothers their opportunities to learn through play. This intruder is television.

Consider these facts. Today, children between the ages of two and five comprise the largest television audience in the United States. In home after home, preschoolers spend over thirty hours a week glued to the TV set. A substantial number watch up to sixty hours of TV a week. To put that figure in full perspective, this means that in many instances virtually all of the young child's waking hours are spent watching television.

As we will show in Chapter Five, steady exposure to the bombardment of TV images stunts the emotional and mental development of young children. Heavy TV viewing can actually retard the development of the child's whole personality and character with far-reaching and perilous consequences to the children involved and to society as a whole.

The early childhood years are, indeed, the crucial years for development. Just as a tree can be dwarfed and twisted in its early years of growth, so can a person's eventual "configuration" be misshapen if normal early patterns of development are seriously interfered with. And a heavy TV diet in the preschool years does just that. It impedes children's normal development by giving them no chance to respond actively and creatively to the stimuli imposed on them, no opportunity to exercise their imaginations, think their own thoughts, play their own games.

How then can we counter the conditions in the outside world and the effect of the TV intruder at home?

If we trace the unfolding of the fascinating powers of play in a young child's life from earliest infancy on, we can see how best to encourage children's innate drive and fantastic ability to play. We can tell when to let children do what comes naturally, how to recognize and satisfy their needs for special play, how to compensate for the familial and social conditions that inhibit creative play.

THE BIOLOGICAL ROLE OF PLAY

To understand the role of play in a young child's life, it helps to start by taking a look at the animal world, at those animals that play and those that do not.

Everybody has seen a kitten playing with a ball of string or watched a puppy worrying a shoe. It's fun to watch the antics of young animals at play, having a great time, much as human children do.

But then there are other animals that don't play at all. Which ones are these? The nonplaying animals are those that are almost ready to be independent, even at birth. Watch a newly hatched chicken. It takes only minutes before it can stand up, scratch the gravel for something to eat and hide under the mother hen's wings when something dangerous approaches. Without having been taught and without having practiced, the chick is independent after a few weeks; soon it is ready to mate and reproduce more of its kind. All the chicken has to do is follow its instincts—which are "programmed" into it by inheritance—to know how to respond to all situations. Unlike puppies, kittens or human children, a chick doesn't need to play because it doesn't need to learn.

The animals that play are the ones that can benefit from experience, that can learn—both step by step and on occasion by leaps of the imagination. The ones that play are those that must learn by discovery and practice, acquiring through trial and error the skills they need to survive.

All intelligent creatures play. The "higher" the animal, the more prolonged is the play phase of life, the more varied and complex the play. In humans, play is *the* primary path to learning for the first five years or so. Ideally, the play-spirit remains as an enriching element in all of our activities throughout our lives. Make-believe games, physical games, play with toys by oneself or with others—all child's play serves the same overall purpose, preparation for adulthood.

How does it all begin? What kind of play and games come first, next, later on? And most important, what aspects of the future adult personality are formed by early play experiences—or by the lack of them?

FIRST GAMES

Play and its power to nurture and to teach begins at birth, in the first interactions between mother and child. In a sense, a baby's own body and his mother's are his first toys. Touching, wiggling, gazing are a baby's first games.

Mealtimes, too, are playtimes. Whether a baby is nursed at his mother's breast or bottle-fed, he sucks most peacefully and contentedly if he is held closely and cuddled in his mother's arms while he is being fed. He sucks, then pauses and looks into her face. He touches his mother's hand, her breast; he wiggles his toes. So it is, too, when a baby is being bathed, changed, picked up or just talked to affectionately. One can see even the youngest infant reaching out with his whole body as if to understand and respond to the playful and affectionate words spoken to him by his parents.

The first important lesson a baby learns is that he is a being apart from his mother. At birth an infant has no awareness of being a unique person, no sense of separateness. But at about eight weeks of age he discovers that his mother's body and his own are not the same. When he sucks his fist, the baby feels something in two different places, his mouth and his hand. When he is being nursed, he has pleasant sensations, to be sure, but only in his mouth. From this he gradually learns that his body encloses the limits of himself. He is his own person, separate and different from all other people.

In being gently, playfully cuddled and caressed, the baby develops what the psychoanalyst Erik H. Erikson calls "basic trust," the predominance of trust over mistrust, the primary goal and achievement of the first stage of human life. According to Erikson's enormously influential concept of the development of character and personality during eight stages of life, the predominance of trust over mistrust is no less than the keystone of identity. Because the baby discovers that a caring person always comes when needed, he gradually develops a trusting response to life that enables him to meet the continuing challenges in the environment and in himself with competence and optimism.

Through playful interchanges with their parents, babies also acquire a basic disposition to feel good about their bodies and the sensations they experience. In truth, this can be said to be the beginning of healthy sex education. The early acceptance of one's body as both a pleasure-giving and a deeply valued part of oneself lays the groundwork for the development of the all-over self respect that later will help the growing child cherish his or her physical, sexual self.

THE LIFE-SAVING
POWERS OF PLAY

It is literally true; playing is as necessary as breathing, eating and sleeping. As surely as children could not survive without air or food, so they could not live very long without play. This, of course, doesn't mean that in order to insure a child's survival his parents should ply him with all sorts of toys or keep admonishing him to go and play "because it's good for you." It does mean, however, that almost from birth parents should—and in the natural course of events, almost all parents do—play with their children. We know how important such early playtimes are because of what happens when adults fail to provide them.

Perhaps the most telling evidence of this fact was discovered almost by chance during the course of a hospital study conducted by a group of researchers working with the eminent psychologist René Spitz. These researchers were exploring the effects of institutional care on infants and young children to see if they could discover why the death rate among babies in orphanages was so tragically high. During the first third or so of this century, years after proper hygienic conditions and adequate nutrition had been established in well-run institutions, there continued to be a very high mortality rate among infants and toddlers in orphanages. At the time of the Spitz study—over twenty years ago—children who had been placed in orphanages during their infancy almost invariably developed severe intellectual and emotional disturbances, becoming either retarded or unbalanced—if, indeed, they lived.

The researchers sought to discover an underlying cause for these tragedies. Was there something in the very nature of such institutions that inevitably handicapped their young inmates—sometimes literally destroyed them? Evidently not, for the psychologists found one orphanage—which, for the purposes of their study, they referred to as Nursery—where the babies and young children were thriving. They then began to compare the children in Nursery with youngsters in another institution, which they called Foundlings Home.

The team was first struck by the fact that by the end of their first year, most of the children in Nursery had developed steadily in keeping with their ages. Their average "developmental quotient" (somewhat similar to an intelligence quotient) increased from 101.5 to 105. They were physically healthy and acted the way children of their age usually do. They had big appetites and enjoyed people. They talked and moved about energetically. By the time they were two, they were running around their quarters, full of laughter and mischief. They could feed themselves. Their weight gain was adequate. They had all the skills of any two-year-old raised at home.

PLAY DEPRIVATION
RETARDS DEVELOPMENT

The children of Foundlings Home were sadly different. They deteriorated under the very eyes of their caretakers; their average developmental quotient decreased from 124 to 72. By the time they were two years old they were like ten-month-old infants. They couldn't walk or talk. They weren't toilet-trained, and hardly any of them could feed themselves. Occasionally, a child would notice that an adult had approached, but this only elicited tears and other signs of fright. The Foundlings Home youngsters were also extremely susceptible to illness. During a measles epidemic, twenty-three out of eighty-eight children died—a much higher than average rate for children in general.

Such a tremendous difference between the children of Foundlings Home and those of Nursery would make one wonder whether the Foundlings Home children came from poorer stock, whether they were genetically inferior. Actually, it was more likely the other way around. In the matter of heredity, the Nursery children probably had several strikes against them, for Nursery was a children's ward attached to a female penitentiary. The children's mothers were young women who had been imprisoned for prostitution. Many of them were classified as mentally retarded. Yet their babies thrived, in marked contrast to the steadily deteriorating babies of Foundlings Home who came from a wide variety of backgrounds and whose inherited traits were likely to be "better" than those of the children in Nursery.

It became clear that what affected the children in both institutions was not nature but nurture. Foundlings Home was far inferior to Nursery in three important respects. First, at Foundlings Home the children had no playthings, in contrast to Nursery where the children were given plenty of toys. Next, each of the Foundlings Home babies had a small cubicle to himself and his own crib, but sheets were hung over the sides of the crib so that each child lived, as it were, in solitary confinement. The Nursery children, on the other hand, were all in a large room. They were able to chatter with one another in their own preverbal way, and their senses were stimulated by what was going on. They saw people coming and going, using all of the things of the everyday world. In other words, the Nursery children had a lot to look at and be aware of; the Foundlings Home children had little, if any, stimulation. The third, and most important, difference lay in the fact that the Nursery children had mothers who came daily to the Nursery from the prison to play with, feed, bathe and cuddle their babies. In Foundlings Home there was only one nurse to take care of eight infants. She scarcely had enough time to feed and bathe the children, never time enough to play with them. This seeming luxury, a caring person to cuddle and play with a child during his first year of life, seals the fate of the young human being. Babies who enjoy loving playtimes learn—and live; the others are fated to vegetate, perhaps to die.

THE IMPORTANCE OF
EXPLORATORY PLAY

As infants grow into toddlers, their play activities bring them increasing command over themselves and their environment. A child has no power over other people or objects until he can get around on his own. Then, characteristically, as the child's horizons widen and his or her powers increase, the youngster begins to discover and handle all sorts of household objects—pots and pans, books, bottles, shoes, knickknacks. All of these can be looked upon as educational toys, except, of course, that they may be fragile, expensive and even dangerous—at any rate, intended for other purposes.

This, then, is the moment when a toddler's overwhelming urge to figure out why things happen and to make things happen—to engage in virtually nonstop discovery play—clashes with his parents' plans for him. They grab him in exasperation and he screams. In these conflicts of interest, parents must insist on their own way. But the adults should bear in mind that their object is not to show the child they are bigger and stronger than he is, and shouldn't be crossed too often—though, of course, this is a secondary lesson that the youngster will be learning. The principal lesson a child learns from such encounters is that there are safe and happy limits to exploration. The child discovers his parents can be trusted and relied on to keep him safe and to show their approval of the achievements that permissible exploration leads to. He learns that though climbing on the bookshelves is forbidden, he can count on his parents to provide something equally attractive and challenging to do instead.

THE INTO-EVERYTHING
TODDLER

Parents should resist indulging in power plays with self-willed toddlers, however aggravating girls and boys of this age can be. The young child who laughs maliciously (the parent can't help feeling) when he throws his spoon on the floor, time after time during the course of almost every meal, may well be teasing his mother. That's learning, too. Mainly, however, he is developing his ability to pick up something, let it go, throw it. He is also discovering that things fall down—not up or sideways—and that they can be picked up and brought back.

By means of all kinds of exploratory, discovery play, boys and girls store up a truly tremendous wealth of important information. They find out, for example, that pillows, sponges and stuffed animals are soft and pleasant to hold, cuddle and rest against; that bathtubs are hard, climbable and make a funny sound when banged; that stairs are steep and bumpy; that cooked cereal is mushy, and you can trace a spoon in its rivers of milk; that a kitchen range can be hot and painful. They learn social lessons, too—that a bigger brother or sister may be friend or foe, sometimes ready to play and protect, at other times a fierce rival for a possession or for Mommy's attention. A toddler can learn even more of life's valuable lessons—about cooperation and competition, the limits of safe aggression and the advantages of harmony—in day-to-day play with a brother or sister than in his relationship with his parents.

All such discoveries made through playing with the people around him and with toys and ordinary household objects are part of what may be called the hidden curriculum of infancy and the toddler stage—the day-to-day experiences that teach optimism, self-confidence, trust, and also caution, fear, wariness.

HOW LOGICAL THOUGHT BEGINS

Some other lessons, too, are hidden in early everyday play. The child learns about time, space and distance—how far it is, in terms of his energy and traveling time, from the crib to the door. He learns that things that have disappeared from sight, such as a series of nesting cups or boxes which vanish inside each other, still exist. This is a lesson of tremendous importance in the child's emotional development (Mommy, too, still exists and can come back even though she's out of sight) and in his intellectual development, as well. Such early learning enhances the capacity to comprehend abstract concepts of size, place and dimension. The child learns everyday lessons in cause and effect, too, through play as he discovers what he can do to things—pulling a toy duck by a string—and what things can do to him—his finger may be pinched by a snapping clothespin.

The remarkable aspect of this sort of learning through play is that it is never lost. Later lessons acquired in school are often forgotten, but the things we learn at play—hard but playfully won—we never forget. All of us recognize that one never really forgets how to ride a bike, say, or throw a ball or any other self-taught, practiced-and-practiced skill, even though the skill may go unused for years. So, too, we never forget the delicious softness of our favorite pillow or the painful bump on the head we got when we crawled under the table. Not that we recall such things consciously, but we have learned for all time about hard tables and soft pillows, and we take their nature for granted on the basis of that early learning. We permit all this knowledge to be dropped into a sort of basement of the mind, where we keep experiences by the trunkload. We don't need to think about them, but we own them just the same; and they determine our actions, not only later on in childhood but in our adult lives, as well.

THE HEALING POWER
OF PLAY

"Last October I suddenly had to fly to Springfield," explains Mrs. Golden. "My father needed to be hospitalized with a heart condition, and since he lives alone, I simply had to go there and check him in. And then I stayed until he was out of danger. Paul and the children stayed home, of course; the two big ones understood the situation very well and were helpful to their father. They also took care of the baby. Judy won't be three for a few months, and no one has ever taken care of her before but me. I always figured she was my last baby and I might as well enjoy her. The night after I left, Kathy, she's ten, gave Judy her supper. Everybody said the baby looked so puzzled and kept asking for me. She was all right, though. Just at mealtimes and when she went to bed, then she kept asking for Mommy.

"That's why I was so surprised and a little upset when I came home. Judy paid absolutely no attention to me. She acted as if I were a stranger. It was hard not to get angry; my feelings were really hurt. She would run toward me as if she wanted to be picked up, but when I opened my arms, she ran away and hid behind the door. She kept playing this game, over and over, for at least a couple of days."

TURNING THE TABLES
THROUGH PLAY

Many children play such games after they have been left in the lurch by their mother or father. They put themselves in the place of the person they love and depend on and who has "deserted" them, as if to say, "I'll show you what it feels like when someone walks out on you. I'll teach you a lesson. This time I am going to be the one who goes away, and you'll be the one who is lonesome and scared."

When a child is hurt or has been wronged by someone, it helps to put himself or herself in the place of the "bad" person, in a make-believe way. As soon as a child feels in command of the situation, instead of being helpless and at the mercy of others, he or she begins to feel much better.

Sometimes it takes much imaginative role-playing to en-able children to master truly frightening situations. That's what happened to four-year-old Peter. A healthy, active child, Peter suddenly became very sick one night. He woke up in great pain and soon began to vomit. Fortunately, the doctor came right away and diagnosed acute appendicitis. Peter was rushed to the hospital and was operated on almost immediately. Medically, all went well and only a week later Peter was back home. His physical recovery was rapid. He had no pain and he could eat everything. He seemed to be in pretty good spirits, too—almost his old self—except for one thing. There was something very strange about his play.

RELIVING PAINFUL
EXPERIENCES

As soon as Peter came home, he began playing "oper-ation". He abandoned his earlier favorite imaginative games, playing race car driver and fireman. All he wanted to do was play "operation" over and over. Every one of his toy animals had its appendix out—many times. He also per-formed mock surgery on his friend Davy.

Though there was no question of hurting anyone or even injuring his toy animals—Peter's surgery was strictly make-believe—his mother became very uncomfortable about the whole thing. So much so that she crossly told Peter to stop playing that way. Wouldn't you suppose, she thought to herself, that Peter would be glad to forget the whole ex-perience? Why did he keep harping on it? Could there be something unhealthy in Peter's response to his operation?

Indeed, Peter's mother was concerned enough to consult a clinical psychologist about her son's behavior. The psychologist was able to put her mind at ease, reassuring her that Peter's reaction was perfectly healthy; actually it was nature's way of restoring Peter to his normally untroubled state.

In fact, Peter would have been all too glad to forget about his appendectomy, and playing "operation" helped him to do just that. One of the most important functions of this kind of reverse role-playing is to help young children assimilate and master shocking or frightening experiences.

The hurried trip to the hospital in the middle of the night, the pain and nausea, the dangerous-looking equipment, the strange people in masks—all these must have been terrifying to Peter. Despite his parents' presence and their explanations of what was happening, Peter must have felt bewildered and utterly helpless, particularly since this was an emergency procedure for which he couldn't have been prepared, as he would have been for a scheduled tonsillectomy. Advance, thoughtful preparation can go a long way toward helping a child cope with the natural anxieties stirred up by such an event. For example, in a reassuring and honest way, the child's parents might begin to tell him about the operation a week or so in advance, describing what the doctors are going to do to make his throat better. A child, like an adult, feels better—in greater control—if he has some idea of what's going to happen and why. A youngster who has been told about his operation, "reads" a picture book about it, visits the hospital beforehand, and knows his mother will be with him when he goes to sleep and wakes up is spared the shock of being thrown unexpectedly into a frightening situation.

But in the absence of such preparation, children help themselves, after the fact, master anxieties by role-playing. So Peter replayed his operation—with one crucial difference. He changed his role from that of powerless victim to powerful person, and thus the event gradually lost its terror and became neutralized. Finally, when it was truly well mastered, it no longer even interested him.

The capacity to overcome the paralyzing power of frightening events by reenacting them and assuming the role of the person in charge is one of the basic functions of imaginative role-playing in early childhood. It is akin to the somewhat compulsive talking-it-out adults do in similar situations—say, Mrs. Smith's recital of the details of her operation told over and over to a captive audience. Though adults do not outwardly play-act away the hurt or anxiety that has been stirred up in them by events such as these, they often need to talk them out. And they "replay" traumatic events in daydreams and while asleep, as well. Like Peter's instinctive play-acting, such measures help people to cope with and master stress, to regain their balance and sense of being in command of themselves and their circumstances.

PROFESSIONAL
PLAY THERAPY

Play is also a useful tool in professional psychiatric therapy with young children. When children show signs of severe emotional distress—for example, having frequent nightmares, engaging in highly aggressive or, conversely, severely withdrawn behavior—play therapy is often the doctor's chief means of uncovering the source of the child's problems and helping the child to overcome them.

Play is a therapeutic tool with young children for several reasons. First, of course, young children do not yet have the mastery of language and abstract thought which enables them to comprehend and discuss their problems, fears and anger. In addition, what emotionally sturdy children do naturally—master fears through imaginative playing—is often difficult or impossible for severely troubled children to accomplish. Their anxiety may be so great as to paralyze their imaginations and inhibit their capacity to play. Thus, the doctor first encourages the child to play, perhaps by literally sitting on the floor and inviting the child to play with dolls, say, or trains, blocks, drawing materials. Then, by observing the nature of the child's play—its themes, patterns, inhibitions, restrictions, repetitions—the doctor gains insight into the child. Play, therefore, becomes the language the doctor must decode. (Of course, play is also the language of emotionally healthy children.) Finally, through the doctor's sensitive guidance and sharing of the child's play, he helps the troubled youngster begin to relieve his anxieties and master his problems.

PREPARATION FOR SCHOOL

Virtually all play in early childhood, whether obviously related to classroom learning or not, is good preparation for school. For example, sandbox play with cups and spoons, measures, sifters and so on is not only fun for all the good, trickly feelings of sand or the satisfying squishiness of mud; it also trains small hands in muscular skills (needed when writing will be taught) develops coordination between eye and hand (also essential for writing) and, yet another bonus, helps to teach concepts such as full, half full, empty, more and less, and so on (all essential to an understanding of addition, subtraction and the other first-learned skills and concepts of arithmetic).

Indeed, not only does such play help to develop intellectual, problem-solving skills; there is much evidence that play is far better preparation for preschoolers in the development of such skills than is specific instruction—say, teaching mathematical skills by means of number or matching games. Among the studies that point up this finding is an experiment conducted a few years ago in a nursery center in Boston. The researchers were Dr. Jerome Bruner, then at Harvard University, now Watts Professor of Psychology at Oxford University, and two of Dr. Bruner's associates at Harvard, Dr. Kathy Sylva and Dr. Paul Genova.

PLAY AND
PROBLEM SOLVING

Three groups of youngsters (nearly 200 children in all), aged three to five, were given a problem to solve: How to get a large piece of colored chalk out of a transparent box that had been placed on a table just out of their reach, without getting out of their chairs. The tools for the task (two sticks and a clamp to join them together) were at hand. The children in one of the groups had a period of free play with sticks and clamps before the experiment began and were shown how a clamp could be fixed to one stick. The second group of children had no initial play period but were given a demonstration of how two sticks could be joined together with a clamp. The third group had no play period and were shown only that a clamp could be fixed to one stick. All three groups were given informative hints during the experiment, such as being asked if they had used everything they could think of that might help them solve the problem. If they still failed to make any progress, the researcher then offered to hold two sticks end to end while asking the children if they could clamp them together.

The results showed that a high proportion of the children in two groups solved the problem without hints. Those who played first and those who saw the principle involved in the solution demonstrated before being given the task, did very much better than the third group. In addition, the children who played first made much better use of the hints than either of the other two groups. And, of greatest importance, the children who played first were more involved (more "goal-directed," as psychologists would put it) in the game. And they clearly viewed the problem as a game. They kept at it. They were more likely than the other two groups to start out with simple, inadequate solutions but to go on steadily to the correct solution. Though more of the children who saw the solution first solved the problem on the first try, many more of those who had played first mastered the problem without hints, after one false start. In discussing the experiment, Dr. Bruner observed, "The children who took the experiment in the spirit of play felt less on the spot... they stuck to the goal more and gave up less easily... in down-to-earth terms, they were happier problem-solvers."

LANGUAGE LEARNING

It is the self-motivation characteristic of true play that carries the child through to the mastery of a task. Nowhere, perhaps, is this more dramatically illustrated than in the young child's acquisition—usually well before the age of four—of basically correct speech, employing a very substantial vocabulary. This is truly a stunning accomplishment; consider how long it takes an adult, who already speaks well and understands the structure of language, to learn a new one.

Although it is impossible to say when a child first begins to learn his native language, one can surely observe the beginning of learning as early as the fourth month or so, when the baby starts to babble, playing with sounds for their own sake. Within a few months the baby has achieved the miracle of associating the sounds made by others and the ones he can make himself with people and objects. Then the first real words are spoken, and from then on children play with speech virtually nonstop.

Dr. Bruner points out in his essay, "Play as a Mode of Construing the Real," "By all odds, the most complex intellectual feat brought off by the young child, his mastery of his native tongue, takes place not under the duress of striving for real goals but in playful situations." Indeed, Dr. Bruner notes, "If you observe the behavior of children just learning to speak, and separate the 'serious' times (when the child could really use better language skills to get what he badly wants) from the less serious times, you will find that it is not in the furnace of necessity but in play that the most daring linguistic hypotheses are generated."

Dr. Bruner is speaking of the way young children (typically during the third year of life) amuse themselves by playing with various kinds of sentences. Talking out loud, often in solitary musings, young children teach themselves the grammar of their language. They practice forming various kinds of sentences, moving from one tense to another, from one mood, say, declarative, imperative or interrogative, to another, and so on.

Linguist Ruth Weir, a research scholar at The Hague, has made recordings of the solitary speech of her two-and-a-half-year-old son just before he falls asleep at night. In addition to sound play—the voicing of rhymes and alliterative words and phrases such as, "Daddy dance, Daddy dance"—she has observed considerable exploration of the rules of sentence structure. She writes that her child's monologues often involve "the selection of a grammatical pattern where substitution occurs in one slot of the grammatical frame... The sequence 'what color, what color blanket, what color mop, what color glass' is an exercise in noun substitution." Another sequence, "go get coffee, go buy some coffee," is, she points out, "an exercise in verb substitution." Altogether, as Dr. Weir observes of her child's musings, "grammar and syntax are considerably practised, so that at times we have the feeling of listening in on a foreign language lesson."

THE CHILD'S NEED
FOR PREDICTABILITY

Through the third year or so, children play in what we might call a wide open way. That is, although they teach themselves almost everything they need to learn, largely through play, they are not yet consciously concerned with the rules or structure of play and games. But by the time girls and boys are about four, their play takes on shape and purpose. Games must have a beginning, a middle and an end. One of the things children learn around this age is that their lives, their worlds, are composed of a logical succession of happenings. Noontime comes after breakfast, bedtime follows supper. Hair is brushed last, after shoes have been put on—if that's the way your preschooler is accustomed to getting dressed. The parent who forgetfully changes this order will be sharply corrected by the child.

Children show a similar stubbornness when it comes to games and play—insisting on following their established routines. The boy who "always" plays on the playground swings is likely to kick up a fuss if his mother wants to take him somewhere else instead.

In storytelling, too, the right order must be followed, as any parent knows who has tried to skip a step or two in the adventures of Goldilocks and the three bears.

Parents and nursery teachers who, in the press of special circumstances, would like to alter a regular daily routine or the way of playing a favorite game would do well not to lose patience with children's reluctance to go along happily with such changes. What boys and girls are really expressing in their stubborn refusal to do things in a new or different way is the need for predictability in their lives and, therefore, for comprehension of their environment. That is what makes a young child feel secure and in command of the small territory he or she inhabits and influences. Thus, what seems like stubbornness is actually a confirmation of the child's growing awareness of the complexity of the world, and an expression of the youngster's attempts to function competently in that world.

This doesn't mean, of course, that adults must never change an accustomed procedure. It does mean that when they do, they should deal responsively with the child's real objections—which are not capricious but are based on genuine need. They should explain why things are being done differently, what will follow from that, and what the benefits of such unusual events are likely to be.

As one sees in the young child's play an awareness of and need for a logical order of events in his daily life—the "way it's supposed to be"—so, too, in play does the child "work over" other aspects of his relationships and experiences.

CHAPTER
II

The Expanding World of Play

REHEARSAL FOR REALITY

PARENTS sometime feel uneasy about a child who engages in a great deal of make-believe play, particularly if the youngster plays with an imaginary person—"the little man who wasn't there"—or with an invisible animal friend. Actually, "pretend" play, including playing with an imaginary friend, is one of the most valuable kinds, perhaps *the* most valuable kind, of play in which preschoolers can engage. Such play develops creativity, intellectual competence, emotional strength and stability—and, wonderfully, feelings of joy and pleasure. The habit of being happy.

Many studies, notably those conducted by Yale psychologists Jerome and Dorothy Singer, show that preschoolers whose play includes a considerable amount of make-believe and fantasy have more advanced language skills than youngsters of equal intelligence (as measured by standardized IQ tests) and perform significantly better in various tasks that call for intellectual reasoning. The Singers point out that imaginative, fantasy play provides the means for children to cope with the intellectual demands, as well as the emotional and social ones, of growing up.

Other developmental psychologists—among them Jerome Bruner, Catherine Garvey of Johns Hopkins University, Lois Barclay Murphy of the Menninger Foundation—have also emphasized the many benefits of imaginative, "let's pretend" play. This kind of play, in which young children act out adult roles—mother, teacher, storekeeper and so on— functions as a safe staging ground to try out various types of behavior the child will need later in real situations. Through pretend-play children begin to fathom the meaning of other people's behavior and to develop comfortable, acceptable styles of behaving themselves. Thus, they begin to acquire genuine self-confidence based on what they have learned through play, as opposed to mere braggadocio, which usually reflects the insecurity born of ignorance.

Jerome Singer has also found evidence that children who engage in a considerable amount of make-believe play are less likely than others to be aggressive and hostile. They are also better able to tolerate frustrations and delays than children who, for whatever reason, do not engage in make-believe games of the imagination. They are better "sharers" with other children, less demanding of their parents and other adults.

An interesting aspect of make-believe play is the parent's role in helping the child develop a tendency to engage in such play. By taking part in a make-believe game suggested by the child—"you sit at the table and I'll be the waiter"—or by beginning a story to which the child can contribute an episode, parents and nursery teachers give their seal of approval to the child's flights of fancy. They set the stage for the full development of the child's powers of imagination, and for his or her delight in using these. Anyone who has played such games with a young child is bound to have observed the richness of the youngster's imagination and his evident pleasure in spinning tale after tale.

Fantasy play includes more than making up situations and roles to act out, or playing with an imaginary friend. It also includes skits and games based on stories that have been read to the child or those he or she makes up based on a popular film or television character. The stories chosen and the roles children assign to themselves tell us a great deal about the concerns of the youngsters at play—and about the times we live in.

DEVELOPING A SENSE
OF SELF

Nowadays, a little girl who picks a story to act out or a character to portray may well choose to be an explorer from *Star Wars* in a daring extraterrestrial exploit rather than acting out the misadventures of Little Red Riding Hood on the way to her grandmother's house. Or, in dramatic play of her own imagining, she may decide to be a doctor or an engineer rather than a housewife and mother or, perhaps, teacher. However, whatever her choice, a little girl today, like her counterpart a generation or two ago, is almost certain to pick a woman to model herself on, not a man.

The many new careers and styles of living now open to both women and men, in reality as well as in TV and film fantasies, are reflected in young children's play. What we witness today, as always, is the desire on the part of preschoolers to model themselves after both real and idealized grown-ups of their own sex. Girls pretend to be women, boys to be men.

This should be reassuring to parents and teachers who fear that encouraging preschoolers of both sexes to play with all manner of toys, at all manner of sports and games, may somehow destroy the basic masculinity of boys, the femininity of girls. Not so. Allowing boys to play with dolls and toy kitchen sets if they chose, without being made to feel like sissies, and permitting girls to have the freedom to play with trucks, fire engines, trains and other "boys" toys, give children of both sexes good opportunities to develop all parts of their personalities more fully.

A HIDDEN PLUS OF
NONSEXIST PLAY

All too many, perhaps most, men and women today have little comprehension of each other—slight awareness that a person of the opposite sex is basically a person like oneself. Even men who are not overly *macho* tend to think of women as different creatures from themselves. In a like vein, most women cannot really appreciate what it's like to be a man, to think or feel like a man. The fact that from early childhood on the male and female paths of socialization increasingly diverge makes it a wonder that men and women ever achieve any real sympathy for each other as humans, let alone as marriage partners.

We are not suggesting that broader play experiences leading to a "rounder" personality will—or should—eliminate the character differences between men and women. On the other hand, we do believe that play experiences that develop so-called boys' traits and skills in girls, and the reverse, may increase the understanding and sympathy between the sexes when the boys and girls are grown up, and may well lessen the misunderstandings, even hostilities, that are all too evident between men and women today.

This story about a little girl we know highlights what is changing and what remains the same in the way children nowadays choose adult models to emulate.

Four-year-old Val and her mother, who is a doctor, were talking about what Val wanted to be when she grew up. "Perhaps you'd like to be a gardener or an artist," Val's mother said, knowing how much her daughter loved to draw and paint and how carefully she tended her plants. "Oh, no, Mommy," Val said with a measure of scorn, "I just want to be a *plain* doctor like you!"

Two things are especially revealing in this story. The first is that little Val takes it for granted that mothers become doctors. Her way of putting it, "a plain doctor", is rather like the unfortunate phrase "just a housewife". Nothing unusual. Nothing special. Of course, both kinds of work are special—and difficult.

The second, very important meaning revealed by this story is that Val's model for her future career is her mother. Occupations change. What mothers do changes. But little girls still want to be like their mothers.

PLAYING ALONE, PLAYING TOGETHER

Children enjoy and benefit from playing in each other's company from the toddler stage on. But the social play of preschoolers is really more of a monologue than a dialogue.

Chip and Michelle, two four-year-olds, are playing together at Michelle's house. Michelle heads for the doll corner of her family's basement playroom as Chip, wearing a red fireman's hat, trails behind her. Michelle goes straight to her doll carriage, in which there are several stuffed animals and dolls. She throws them all out except for a kitten with a pink sunbonnet, which seems to be her favorite and which she tenderly tucks in under the blanket. Michelle begins wheeling the buggy around and around, as if to take the kitten for a walk. Chip watches it all from under his hat. Michelle says to Chip, "You be her Daddy. I'm the Mommy. Come on, Daddy, it's time for dinner." Chip frowns and says, "Can't. Got to put out the fire." He waves expansively, climbs into a cardboard box, pretends to turn a steering wheel, then, making the loudest, most piercing sounds he can, he turns on a pretend siren.

Michelle, busy doing her own thing, pays no attention. "C'mon baby, it's time to eat." She kisses the kitten's nose, seats it in a high chair at the table and starts setting three places—plates, spoons, cups. Next, Michelle picks up a piece of clay, sniffs it, squashes it, pounds and slices it. She puts a piece of clay on the kitty's plate and says rather sternly, "There. Eat your hamburger." Then she picks up the kitten and scolds her angrily. "What, again. That baby wet her pants again! And she spilled her milk. I'm gonna throw her out of the window!" She slaps the kitty, then checks herself and says soberly, "You go to bed now. You were a bad girl." She gives the kitty another pat, but a softer one, and puts it back into the doll carriage. Looking pleased with herself, as if to say, "I've done my job well. I'm in charge here," Michelle walks over to the other side of the room where Chip is.

TRYING OUT
ADULT ROLES

Two interesting aspects of children's needs and development can be seen in this typical situation. First, as we noted before, Michelle chooses a woman's role, Chip a man's, to play-act. What about Michelle's choice? Does her quickness to spank the kitten mean she's going to grow up to hit her children and be an abusive mother? Not likely. Michelle's play reveals that what impresses her most about grown-up women is that they take charge: they're smart and competent. They're in command, and they have it in their power to be kind and forgiving as well as to be strict. This is how

Michelle envisions herself in the future. She wants to be like the woman she knows best, her mother.

Obviously Chip doesn't model himself after his father, as Michelle does after her mother, almost certainly because he hasn't enough "raw material" to work with. He doesn't know enough about the details of his father's job to play-act it, so he chooses, instead, material he knows from stories he's heard about strong and heroic men. Like Michelle, what Chip is practising to be is the kind of adult who is in control, someone you can rely on and admire.

As children grow and develop, and their interests become increasingly specialized, their goals for themselves may be substantially different from their parents' way of life. But the earliest wish remains—to become as competent as their first, all-powerful protectors.

THE BEGINNING
OF FRIENDSHIP

What we see in the children's skits, which are really two congruent but not overlapping plays, is the beginning of companionship. Children of this age have reached a kind of prefriendship stage. They are still too egocentric, too occupied in developing their own sense of self to be able to fathom another child's thoughts or respond sympathetically to another child's needs. The capacity for real friendship—that is, the ability and willingness to identify with another person—is still several years in the future. During the preschool years, children gradually get the feel of others. By observation and by accommodating themselves to the external demands made on them (to share their toys and "play nicely" with each other) they develop prerequisites for true friendship.

ANIMAL PLAYMATES

Pets can be particularly valuable to children still too young to derive the emotional sustenance that comes with real friendships, shared feelings, shared identification. An animal playmate serves the child as a confidant, joins in his adventures, offers him solace in times of defeat or unhappiness.

Not surprisingly, therefore, almost every young child yearns to have a pet. The same, however, cannot always be said of parents, especially if the family lives in a small apartment. The parents may point out, quite correctly, that millions of children have grown up to be perfectly well-adjusted adults without ever having had a dog or cat, or even a goldfish. So why bother? Yet when reluctant parents do consent to "adopt" a pet, the animal usually becomes deeply beloved by all members of the family.

Many parents who accede to a child's request for a pet do so principally because they believe that having a dog or cat will teach the youngster to be responsible. Such parents are likely to be disappointed. A sense of responsibility can't be acquired overnight; it develops only gradually. At ten or twelve some children will be mature enough to be in charge of another creature, but preschoolers and young school children can't be expected to regularly feed a dog or cat, and certainly not to take a pet out for a walk, on a daily schedule.

The real value of a pet is as a playmate, one that offers the child a special kind of mirror in which to view himself. A pet is always there, always loyal, whether the child has been good or bad, shared his toys with his little sister or grabbed them away, remembered to tidy up his room or sulked and shouted at his mother.

Young children want their pets to join in their play and games; they really don't understand why King doesn't like chewing gum or Mittens hates to be dressed up like a doll and wheeled around in a carriage. But then, like their pets, young children don't bear grudges and are always eager to include them in their next games. Indeed, children are happy to play the kind of games, like catch and Frisbee, that their pets enjoy the most.

A preschooler may become very fond of a dog, so fond, in fact, that the youngster's mother may feel a bit jealous of the animal. When Grandpa gave Hank a beagle for his birthday, Hank's mother said, "I was certainly all for it. I thought it would teach him to be responsible. We told him this was his dog and he would absolutely have to help take care of him. Well, he does, sometimes, at least as much as I can expect him to. But for me it's like having another child to look after. I don't even mind that. What I do mind is that I seem to be losing the closeness I had with my first child. Hank has really changed; he lavishes affection on the dog, but he won't even kiss me in front of company."

PETS PROVIDE A SAFETY VALVE
FOR FEELINGS

What Hank's mother doesn't realize is that the chances

are he wouldn't have behaved very differently toward her even if he didn't have a new beagle. By the age of four or so, many boys are beginning to be embarrased about showing affection toward their parents in the presence of strangers. Hugging and kissing make them feel squeamish; they think they should be more grown up and manly. But a child of this age still needs a great deal of physical closeness, and if he's growing ashamed to ask for—or accept—it from his parents, he can, without suffering in his own eyes, show his affectionate feelings toward his dog.

Pets can be a great asset to children's development in another way. Consider the daily routine of a young child. It is likely to be shot through with all kinds of demands and restrictions, ranging from "stop making so much noise," to "put your toys away before you go out," to "must you always fight with your sister?". This state of affairs is nobody's fault. Children have to learn to live with others, and parents are the ones who must teach them how. Therefore, parents nag from time to time; at least, that's how children view it. Here, too, a dog or a cat can supply what human beings can't—total approval. A child's pet shows that he feels the youngster is lovable, indeed, perfect, when nobody else does. Having a pet who loves him unconditionally teaches a child something tremendously important—that the child is truly worthwhile. A pet that can be counted on is not only a child's best friend, it is also one of the most reliable allies parents have in their job of raising their children to be emotionally stable and secure.

PLAY FOR THE
HANDICAPPED CHILD

As we can see, play is a prime means to full development for everyone—and most particularly for boys and girls who are mentally or physically handicapped. Through play, especially shared play with caring family members and friends, even severely retarded or handicapped children can make truly miraculous gains.

For too long in our society we have hidden away the handicapped—behind closed doors at home and often in institutions. As a society and as individuals, we have averted our eyes from unpleasantness and from the necessity we might feel to do something about the plight of handicapped people if we saw them daily. We so-called normal people have not wanted to afflict ourselves with the sight of the afflictions of others.

Individual parents are hardly to blame. Parents whose children have been handicapped physically, mentally or both, as is often the case, by inheritance, birth injury, or an illness or accident after birth, have all too often been told there is nothing that can be done to help their children. And so, overcome by a sense of helplessness and frequently by guilt or shame—unable to devise ways to build a good family life or help the handicapped child—parents have allowed children who could live and prosper at home to be placed in institutions, supposing that it was best for them. Sometimes there is no choice, but often children and older people, too, who might function well at home, in school and in the community if the proper support and information were given to their families, remain in institutions.

Increasingly, it is being discovered that virtually all handicapped people have much more potential than we might have supposed, and that the high road to the achievement of that potential lies in shared play activities.

THE MYTH
OF NORMALITY

Actually there is no such thing as a normal child or adult or, for that matter, normal development. There are only averages. Handicapped and normal are words we use to describe certain qualities of one kind or another. All of us are both, and neither.

There is probably no one alive who does not carry genes for one or several defects. Sometimes these are hidden, or recessive, genes and the defects do not show up in us but may very likely turn up in our children. And many of us have defects that would probably be apparent under close scrutiny and would be handicapping to one degree or another except that without ever having been aware of it, we managed to compensate for the defects during our childhood.

HOW PLAY WORKS TO
HELP THE HANDICAPPED

Many of the skills that develop as a matter of course by means of spontaneous play in most youngsters can be taught through guided play and games to handicapped children.

With the simplest of equipment—for example, a length of

plastic rope, blocks and nesting cups, a squeezable sponge ball small enough to fit into a young child's hand, a large "beach" ball strong enough to bear the child's weight—parents can embark on a whole series of games with the handicapped child that can markedly enlarge the child's strength, coordination, competence and understanding.

Games help the handicapped, not only because they develop physical and mental skills but because they "reach" the handicapped as no other activities can when they are performed in a playful spirit. Handicapped children, even the severely mentally retarded, have feelings like anybody else. When they are left out of family activities, when no one plays with them, they can only become more isolated, frustrated and incompetent.

For a handicapped child, play not only provides the foundation for later learning as it does for all children, it can also open the way to some of the relatively few careers suitable for the handicapped. We know of children with Down's Syndrome who are gymnastic instructors for other handicapped children, having first learned themselves to become competent gymnasts through the "Let's Play to Grow" program developed by the Joseph P. Kennedy Jr. Foundation in Washington, D.C.

We have also seen physically handicapped recreational therapists at a Massachusetts state hospital who gained skills themselves and learned how to help others by means of physical play therapy programs in clinics and in their homes.

For a handicapped child, the joy born of each new accomplishment is itself a spur to further accomplishment and to the happiness and sense of self-worth all children deserve to experience.

(See the Bibliography, page 117, for materials on play and games to help handicapped children.)

CHAPTER
III

What Makes a Good Nursery School

Nursery school can be a superb place for young children, offering them an environment for rich and varied play that could never be provided at home. A nursery school can enhance children's development and bring them the joy of feeling ever greater self-reliance and success. That is, a good nursery school can do all this. By "good" we mean one that permits plenty of time for imaginative play by oneself, in pairs or small groups; time and space for active physical play; and time, too, for just resting, alone.

PLAY VERSUS LESSONS

Unfortunately, many nursery schools set up structured classrooms to teach reading and math—actual lessons, though often disguised as games or play. Such lessons, in our view, are a waste of time. The Swiss psychologist Jean Piaget, whose pioneering observations of young children were begun half a century ago, has made this point succinctly. "Every time we teach a child something, we keep him from inventing it himself. On the other hand, that which we allow him to discover by himself, will remain with him visibly...for the rest of his life."

Indeed, this is the wisdom of the ages. In discussing the kind of education young children need to prepare them to become the leaders in a just society, Plato cautioned in *The Republic* that one should "avoid compulsion and let early education be a sort of amusement. Young children learn by games; compulsory education cannot remain in the soul."

Among the current studies comparing the value of imaginative play with structured games designed to teach school-related cognitive skills are several conducted recently in Israel by Dr. Dina Feitelson of the University of Haifa. She notes that a large portion of the usual nursery school curriculum is devoted to developing skills supposed to be essential to learning to read, "exercises in visual and auditory discrimination, learning letter names, tracing and copying letters and words, along with the use of audio-visual equipment and work-books."

In a paper presented at the Child Advocacy Conference, held in the summer of 1979 at Yale University, Dr. Feitelson observed of this kind of curriculum, "not only has serious research failed to show marked benefits, but some of these practices may even do more harm than good." An experiment she recently conducted showed that "certain types of play may well be more effective in developing pre-reading skills than the paper and pencil tasks so often used for this purpose."

WHAT RESEARCH SHOWS

In one of Dr. Feitelson's studies, matched pairs of preschoolers from three widely different environments (an Arab village, a small-city housing development, and a middle-class neighborhood in Haifa) attended eight preschool sessions in which they were evenly divided into groups of four. The children were either tutored to use the reading worksheets recommended by the Department of Early Education in Israel, or given puzzles, mosaics and blocks to play with. All of the children were then asked to perform an assigned task—to copy a five-word sentence with a set of movable letters. Dr. Feitelson observed that in all of the groups, the children who had the opportunity to play "made significantly fewer mistakes than those who had been exposed to reading-readiness teaching." Moreover, "The children in the worksheet groups became increasingly disaffected. While those in the toy groups looked forward most willingly to their sessions, considerable pressure had to be exerted in the worksheet groups to make them continue to the final session. Actually, they consented to do so only on the promise that they, too, would be allowed access to the toys."

In spite of findings that cast serious doubt on the value of teaching reading and math readiness lessons in nursery schools, many parents and educators alike continue to promote this formal curriculum. They are motivated, in the one case, by the desire to have their children move upward in the world (through school success), and in the other, by the belief that our nation as a whole has become deficient in the way it trains its young people to acquire the "hard" skills of math and science (a fear we have been harboring since the Russians launched Sputnik). In both cases, parents and educators have supposed that the way to raise a family or, for that matter, a nation of intellectually vigorous and knowledgeable men and women is to begin at the earliest possible moment with lots of "hard" teaching, sometimes masquerading as play in the form of games.

LEEWAY WITHIN LIMITS

In arguing the merits of imaginative exploratory play over more formally structured lesson-games, we do not mean to suggest that the ideal nursery school is completely unstructured. Of course, there should be predictably scheduled activities to meet the preschool-age child's need to feel the confidence that comes from understanding what's going to happen next and what the world is all about. But the activities should provide the children with the time and opportunity to give free rein to their imaginations. A curriculum which paces the children in lockstep, fifteen minutes for storytelling, fifteen minutes for artwork, fifteen minutes for play on the swings and slides, seems too regimented to us.

What kind of scheduling, then, best satisfies children's needs for both freedom and structure? It is impossible to define exactly the best mix of free play and planned activities. Different children have different needs at different times.

It is likely, for example, that by the age of four, or so, an only child will have learned to rely more on his own imagination than a child who has never had much time alone. Though deriving much satisfaction from fantasy play, such a child may yearn for the chance to team up with others in structured, organized games, played according to the rules at a scheduled time.

Understandably, experts differ considerably about how much playtime should be truly free and unstructured. But all warn against extremes in devising a preschool curriculum. Neither anarchy nor regimentation meets the developmental needs of preschoolers. We know empirically that between the ages of two and a half and five children are highly volatile in their emotions and their behavior. They are still unable to control their moods or their actions, which can swing from one extreme to another in a very short space of time. They cannot sit still long enough to study or concentrate on a subject, particularly at someone else's bidding. That comes later—usually by the age of five and a half or six—when children are better able to understand and conform to the demands of others rather than to their own feelings. Then they are ready for learning by means of more formal teaching rather than principally by self-directed play.

In sum, the ideal nursery school encourages children to use their imaginations in active play and daydreaming, and it offers, as well, opportunities for organized games, including vigorous outdoor play. But there is no merit, and considerable danger, in including in the curriculum lesson-games designed to teach children reading skills and abstract mathematical concepts.

THREE KEYS TO
SCHOOL READINESS

Even the ideal play school is not right for every young child. Three broad factors should be taken into account in deciding whether or not going to nursery school will be a plus for a particular child. The first is the child's age or, really, stage of development. The second is the parents' expectations, hopes and concerns for their child. And the third is the particular circumstance of the child's life at the time nursery school is being considered.

First, the youngster's age and stage of development. What is the ideal age for a child to attend nursery school? Generally speaking, we believe it is three or four years old. Why wait until three? Why do we think that, on the average, a child of two or even two and a half is probably too young to derive much benefit from going to nursery school? It is true that younger children are natural explorers and adventurers (and a good nursery school satisfies this need for exploration and discovery), but they are still very dependent on their mother's presence as a kind of background figure or resource person to run to—in pride at an accomplishment, for reassurance at a setback.

Though toddlers usually don't need their mothers right on the scene with them all of the time, they do need to know

where she is and that they can check in with her from time to
time. Children of this age do not usually yet have the power
of mind to understand the meaning of a temporary separation. A two-and -a-half-year-old may have been told that his
mother will be back at noon—in just three hours—but
this makes no sense to him. He thinks the time will never
pass and, consequently, he isn't free to relax and enjoy
himself at play, to throw himself wholeheartedly into any
particular activity. Instead, his energies are taken up by
worry. And so, what would otherwise be an all-too-short
morning of adventure seems like an eternity. A painful and
empty eternity.

WHEN NURSERY CARE IS A MUST

All the same, many parents have no choice but to place a
youngster under three in a nursery school or day-care
center. The mother or father in a one-parent household
usually must be at work all or a good part of the day. And in
many families both parents must work to earn enough
money for their needs. Over a third of the mothers in the
United States with children under three now have full-time
jobs, and many of them must send their young children to a
nursery center. Naturally, they're likely to worry about the
effect on the children of such an all-day, every-day, separation from them.

Mothers worry, in particular, that they will lose the child's
love, that he may come to need and prefer his teacher. But
studies by psychologists show that even when day care
begins in infancy, the child's primary emotional tie to his
mother need not be disrupted.

One such study was conducted by psychologists Dale C. Farran and Craig Ramey of the Frank Porter Graham Child Development Center of the University of North Carolina at Chapel Hill. Drs. Farran and Ramey set up an experiment with the children in the Center's own model day-care program. The children were between the ages of nine months and two-and-a-half years, and all of them had been in the program—for all-day, five-day-a-week care—since they were three months old.

To evaluate the impact of day care on the children's attachment to their mothers, the researchers brought the children, one at a time, into a room to play. There were plenty of toys, and the child's regular teacher with whom he or she was comfortable was there. Also present was a man the child had never seen before and the child's own mother, who, of course, was normally not present in nursery school.

The researchers took note of the child's approaches to each of the adults—the mother, the teacher, and the stranger—how often and how close the child came to the adult, to whom the child turned for companionship or help. All of the children invariably went to their mothers first rather than to either of the other two adults when they had something to show them, or if they needed help or comfort.

Questions of children's physical health, and social and intellectual progress also concern parents considering nursery care for toddlers and preschoolers. Studies show that although the incidence of colds and minor upsets is greater among children at nursery school than among those cared for at home, the incidence of serious illness is not.

As for social behavior, some studies indicate that children who have attended nursery school regularly from an early age are more aggressive, less compliant, than other young-sters, very likely because the give-and-take in a nursery school helps children to become strong-willed and inde-pendent. However, parents should consider these findings in the light of their own values. Parents who prize inde-pendence and assertiveness may welcome an environment for their children that helps to develop these qualities.

What about the effect of nursery school on children's intellectual development? As we have tried to show, this is a question that has been too strongly—and wrongly—em-phasized by parents and professionals alike. Aside from the fact that imaginative playing—in a nursery setting or else-where—is the best way for young children to learn, it seems to us that developing children's intellectual and school skills should not be the prime goal of parents and teachers. Much more important is providing an environment in which a child can be happy—now.

In modern times we have learned to think, correctly, of childhood as a process, a stage on the way to adulthood. Unfortunately, however, many parents and educators have fixed their attention so firmly on the end goal of the process—adulthood—that they have neglected to give enough consideration to the child as he or she is now—to the child's right to enjoy life at the moment.

In any case, there is no evidence that attending nursery school has any lasting effect on children's intellectual de-velopment one way or the other. Though a child who has little or no chance for playful interactions at home may make more rapid progress in a comfortable, stimulating good school than he would at home, there is no evidence that such gains will be lasting.

HOW TO CHOOSE
A NURSERY SCHOOL

To sum up, parents who are looking for a school or a day-care center should visit the setting, talk to the people in charge, observe the general tone of the place and how the children seem to be responding to it. It's also a good idea to talk to the parents of children attending the school and, if possible, to the parents of recent "graduates" to get their impressions, too. The following checklist should be helpful to parents.

Number of Teachers. The children should be looked after by the same adult day after day and not by a changing cast of characters. However, there should be, at least from time to time, more than one adult available; taking care of even a few children for long hours each day can be physically and emotionally exhausting.

Maturity. The teacher should be sufficiently experienced and mature to take care of the children without feeling deprived or resentful at having to put their needs above her own.

Responsibility. It is essential that the teacher be reliable, consistent and predictable. Of course, everybody has good days and bad days, but the teacher's mood swings should not be excessive.

Affection and Discipline. The teacher should be kind and affectionate, and she or he should show such feelings. However, the teacher must also be able to discipline the children, not on the basis of his or her own moods, but when the children's behavior requires it.

Enthusiasm. The teacher should be a lively and enthusiastic person. Whatever she especially enjoys—baking, reading, gardening, playing music—her eagerness to try new things will be contagious, encouraging the children's curiosity and initiative.

Scheduling and Orderliness. There should be a fairly predictable sequence of events. Meals should be served on schedule; ample time should be regularly provided for free play, storytelling and other group activities, such as dancing and singing. Regular time should also be set aside for a rest period. The room or rooms should appear reasonably well-organized but should not look unnaturally tidy.

Facilities and Equipment. Although fancy surroundings and equipment are neither necessary nor particularly desirable, there should be basic tools for both indoor and outdoor play. Indoors there should be spaces set aside for different kinds of play: an area for playing with blocks and construction toys; a quiet corner for resting and "reading," well-stocked with picture books and magazines. A kitchen corner with child-sized kitchen equipment is desirable, an art center with paper, crayons, paints, clay and other supplies is a must.

Various child-powered action toys—trucks and wagons and musical toys—are also essential basic equipment. Outdoors there should be space enough and sufficient equipment for active running, jumping and climbing games. Slides, swings, jungle gyms and facilities for ball playing should be available.

SEPARATION ANXIETY

Sometimes a child who gives every indication of being ready to profit from the rich and varied opportunities for play that a good nursery school provides becomes distressed at going, obviously frightened at the thought of being separated from his mother.

Separation anxiety, as psychologists call it, is often felt by the "only" child whose mother has hovered over him or her too much—worrying that something terrible will happen to the child the minute she's out of sight. Such overprotection on a mother's part may stem from, or at least include, her resentment at being tied down. She feels overburdened and, hiding such feelings from herself, she overcompensates by trying to take particularly good care of the child.

If this makes such a mother sound unnatural, it shouldn't. Almost all parents partake, in some measure, of feelings like these. The trouble comes when we try to hide our feelings from ourselves because we feel guilty—ashamed of wishing we could sometimes be relieved of the all-day responsibility of looking after a child.

And, of course, there is a fine line between protecting and overprotecting; the streets outside our homes are often hazardous places for children to play, so it's natural to worry about a young child when he's out of sight. But letting our children see that we are anxious about them and are doubtful of their capacities undermines their confidence in themselves and may make them terrified to go off on their own.

Interestingly enough, children who have been overprotected and, as a consequence, are afraid to go anywhere without their mothers aren't necessarily afraid for themselves.

A four-year-old youngster who is reluctant to go to school may be mainly apprehensive about what's happening to his mother in his absence. He feels this way partly because if something should happen to his mother—his chief protector—then he will be alone and helpless. Also, a mother who unconsciously resents her role is likely to transmit that message, however subtly, to her child, making him feel that her continued love and protection are not securely his.

A.A. Milne characterizes this syndrome in his charming verse, "Disobedience," which begins:

"James, James
Morrison Morrison
Weatherby George Dupree
Took great
Care of his Mother
Though he was only three
James James
said to his Mother,
"Mother," he said, said he:
"You must never go down to the end of the town
if you don't go down with me."

And those of us who remember our Milne know what happened to Mrs. Weatherby George Dupree. Ignoring her son's cautions, she *did* go down to the end of the town without him, and—*"Has never been heard from since."*

CUTTING THE APRON STRINGS

This doesn't mean that a youngster who is overly dependent on his mother shouldn't go to nursery school. The boy who insists his mother stay nearby when he plays in the yard or who won't go off to the playground with the other kids needs to develop the independence a nursery school can foster. But parents who have been overprotective should first make an effort to help the child broaden his or her horizons by encouraging the child to try new things, perhaps suggesting errands and chores that call for competence and independence of judgment. Parents might also encourage visits that the boy or girl can make without them—for example, taking the youngster for an overnight visit to a friend's home. Parent and child together might also make a game of role-playing going-away situations—to nursery school itself, or on trips. Pretend plane and train travel, for example, is the kind of role-playing children love. A child who has traveled by air is sure to surprise and amuse an adult by his imagination and his acute observation as he imitates the pilot's voice that comes over the loudspeakers, the stewardess, the other passengers.

Pretend-play allows lots of room for the parent to suggest scenes in which the child is on his own for a while—for example, while his mother goes to buy the tickets. Acting out how he might feel and what he should do if he should lose sight of his mother or stray away from where he was supposed to wait gives the youngster a chance to work out good solutions in advance to situations he may face in the real world.

Why bother? Shouldn't a fearful child just stay home? We think it's well worth the effort to cope with separation anxiety constructively and positively early. A fearful child is not a happy child, and if these first roots of fear are left to grow unchecked, then the habit of being afraid, of feeling like nobody unless you have someone around for protection, can crop up in many ways, time and again, all through the years. So, the first cause of what could be a lifelong tendency to separation anxiety—a lack of trust in oneself and the fear of being abandoned—should be dealt with in early childhood.

WHEN GOING TO NURSERY SCHOOL SHOULD BE POSTPONED

Even generally outgoing children who are not prone to separation fears but are well-prepared to enjoy and profit from attending a nursery school may find it difficult under certain circumstances.

All summer long, three-and-a-half-year-old Sarah had been looking forward to going to nursery school, particularly because as the time approached for the new baby's birth, her mother seemed to be too tired to play with her as much as she used to. Mommy wasn't cranky or mean, but she did seem abstracted, as if her thoughts were somewhere else a lot of the time.

Sarah's mother had talked to her about how much fun it would be to have many children to play with in nursery school, and Sarah seemed eager to start in the fall.

But when September came, though everything was fine with her just-born baby brother, Sarah was acting unlike herself. She had started school eagerly enough, but more and more often when it was time to go to school, she cried and didn't want to leave. When she was at home, she didn't play the let's-pretend games she used to make up with such delight, and she didn't want to play with the children in the neighborhood, either.

Still, it didn't occur to Sarah's mother that her daughter was jealous of the baby. For one thing, Sarah's mother had taken pains to prepare her daughter for the baby's birth. For another, Sarah didn't act jealous. She didn't show resentment toward the baby or suggest as a neighbor's first-born had after a brother was born, that they take the baby right back to the hospital. Actually, Sarah seemed to love her brother and was always eager to help her mother—to hand her the can of talcum powder or rock the baby in his carriage. The only thing that was different about Sarah was her reluctance to go to school and the fact that she didn't enjoy playing alone or with others the way she used to.

But, of course, Sarah was jealous. That's why she was afraid to go to school or play with her friends. At home she could stick close to her mother, and make sure she was still needed and valued by being as helpful as possible.

The first feelings of jealousy, which stem from a fear of being displaced, can wear many faces. Jealousy can be shown in outburts of temper and open resentment of the new baby, or in regression to infantile behavior—wanting a bottle or wetting one's bed like the baby. A jealous child may begin to have bad dreams and be afraid to go to bed at night. Or, as in Sarah's case, jealousy can be revealed by the child's attempt to make sure he or she is still needed—and by an alteration in the child's usual play behavior.

Indeed, in any circumstances, one of the signs that a child may be troubled is a sudden and dramatic change in the youngster's style of playing. A child whose inner energies are taken up by anxiety is likely to reveal this either in the way he plays (as we saw in the case of the little boy who played and replayed his operation), or in an inability to feel relaxed enough to play at all.

So this wasn't a good time to start nursery school, even for a usually self-reliant child. It would have been better for Sarah to have started school a month or two earlier, well before the baby was born. Then she would not have felt she was being sent away to make room for the baby. Or, since that was not possible, going to school should have been postponed until Sarah felt more secure again, more used to the baby's presence and his routines—to the time when the baby became taken for granted as a member of the family.

There are other times, too, when it's not a good idea for a child to begin going to nursery school—when there is an illness in the family, for example. If a child's mother has been sick, the girl or boy is likely to view starting school as being sent away, very likely as a punishment for having been bad, maybe even for having caused the parent's illness. In general, it's best not to start something new in a child's life, especially something that involves going away from home, at times of change or crisis in the family.

CHAPTER
IV

Worrisome Play

CERTAIN kinds of perfectly natural play strike many parents and teachers as downright unhealthy and dangerous. Aggressive play, in particular, troubles many adults. Parents become quite distressed when their children get into fights; they worry that something may be wrong with their children's basic characters.

Not just aggressive play but play with a distinct sexual component may upset even the coolest of parents. And so frequently, though usually to a lesser degree, do daydreaming and fantasy play. But these kinds of play are natural expressions of children's exploratory drive, which, if properly channeled, promote healthy growth.

79

WHAT TO DO
ABOUT AGGRESSION

Stella Harrison had begun to take her four-year-old daughter, Meg, to the playground a couple of times a week. Meg liked to play in the sandbox and on the slides and swings, and she especially enjoyed playing with Jill, a little girl her own age who also came to the playground with her mother two or three times a week. One day, as Meg and Jill were playing contentedly, deeply engrossed in baking sand pies, Meg suddenly hauled off and slapped Jill—hard—on the cheek. Jill hardly knew what had hit her. She didn't cry; she just sat there open-mouthed and wide-eyed. But Meg's mother was horrified, and she yanked her daughter out of the sandbox. "How could you be so mean?" she demanded. "Why did you hit Jill? She didn't do anything to you."

Meg, unperturbed, answered as if it were the most natural thing in the world, "I had to. I had to hit her back, first."

We adults recognize, all too well, the principle of hitting back first. Meg's candid and straightforward description strikes us as funny because it reminds us of our own tendencies toward "defensive" behavior—in the business world, in politics, in social relationships. We laugh because we're ashamed. Meg wasn't ashamed, because she meant no real harm.

Her action—impulsive, unpremeditated—probably surprised her as much as it did her playmate, who took it quite in her stride. Indeed, after the scolding, Meg and Jill resumed playing as if nothing at all had happened. The incident seemed forgotten, but not by Meg's mother. She was truly upset by what she had witnessed. What had gotten into Meg? She had never done anything like that before.

Where does the aggressive element, which is present in virtually all play and games, come from?

THE DIFFERENCE BETWEEN AGGRESSION AND HOSTILITY

Aggression starts with life itself and serves an essential biological function. The earliest exploratory play of every infant has an aggressive character. The intensity with which a baby searches for and latches onto the nipple, the forceful way in which even a tiny baby waves his arms, flexes his legs, thrusting down hard against his mother's lap as if to stand up long before he can stand or even sit—such actions are aggressive. But this kind of aggression—the consequence of a biological drive—is not the same as hostile aggression. Though aggression may make an impact, sometimes an unpleasant one, on another person, aggression itself is not necessarily hostile, even when it is in a true sense de-structive. Rather, it is the same life-force that makes a seedling push upward, a young bird peck its way out of the shell and forage for food, a big fish devour a little fish or a cat consume a mouse. Aggression is a lifelong component of all play, learning and work. It is the force behind our highest achievements as well as our most terrible acts. Aggression can be expressed constructively or destructively, but it is only truly hostile when its principal aim is to injure someone or something.

CHANNELING AGGRESSION
SAFELY

If the aggression in children's behavior is not injurious to the child or to others, and if aggressive play is not the main and only way in which a youngster plays, it is nothing to worry about. Rather, it is a sign that the child has an urge to prevail, to find out, to test himself. In other words, aggressive play promotes development. This doesn't mean that punching another child is recommended. Obviously, it should be discouraged, but unless it is habitual it's not necessary to respond as intensely as Meg's mother did. Meg is only beginning to find out what to do with the surplus energy that led her to hit out, more in exploration than in anger. Four-year-olds who play together are used to rough and tumble. Punching or hitting among young children is not nearly as likely to indicate hostility as fighting is among older children or adults.

TOYS AND VIOLENCE

Play with toy guns and other weapons is extremely upsetting to a great many parents and teachers today who fear that such play promotes violence and even war.

Mrs. Hastings, a nursery school teacher and a warm and peace-loving person, was bothered by the gunslingers in her room. As the toy armaments in her classroom increased in number, she became more troubled and decided to take a firm stand. She explained to the children why guns were bad, that they killed people, and that from now on there were to be no more guns in class. Not even water pistols. The children listened attentively; some nodded agreement and the guns disappeared.

But the next morning Mrs. Hastings found herself faced with a classroom of children pointing plastic forks and crayons at each other while they made rat-a-tat machine gun noises. What was Mrs. Hasting to do? Confiscate the forks and crayons? She realized that if she took these away another substitute would soon be found. She decided to accept—and ignore—the children's need for gunplay. Within a few weeks, most of her charges had tired of make-believe shoot-outs in favor of less warlike games.

Pretend gunplay or, indeed, any kind of role-play does not indicate a propensity to violence or foreshadow a particular kind of career, least of all a criminal one. Certainly not for children who have caring and conscientious parents who offer their children affection, encouragement—and discipline, too. A badly neglected and brutally treated child, on the other hand, does not need toy guns to harbor serious thoughts of destructiveness and, perhaps, one day to act on them in reality.

SIBLING RIVALRY

A special instance of aggression with a considerable component of hostility, rivalry between siblings, is probably the single aspect of child behavior that depresses and fatigues parents the most. And worries them the most, too.

It is sometimes hard to define the difference between a mere game between siblings that involves "torturing" the "victim" and dangerously hostile behavior. More often than not, parents don't know whether or not to interfere in their children's fights. Is it best to scold their youngsters and drag them apart, or just wait it out and let the kids settle their squabbles by themselves?

Parents who are brave enough to leave the room when hostilities start (a step we would not advise unless the children are at least three or four years old) find that retreating from the battle scene almost invariably stops a sibling fight before it gets out of hand.

When parents notice the beneficial effects of their absence, they may wonder how it would be if they were not in reach at all. What about having their children's play supervised by someone else? Would the kids engage in such battles over the doll house, the toy truck, the building blocks?

The answer is, they probably wouldn't. Even siblings who are usually at each other's throats in the family circle are likely to react to the absence of their parents by closing ranks and loyally protecting each other.

Yet, prolonged absences of the parents would, in the long run, make it harder for the children to learn to get along with each other—learn to love one another. For it isn't each other's possessions they're really fighting over, they're battling for their parents' approval, attention, interest. Until they feel that need is satisfied, they are bound to snipe at each other.

Every experienced parent knows that the minute a child is alone with one parent the youngster is willing to compromise about the things he was adamant about the moment before. Almost all children are like that. Jealous kids are in a sense paying a compliment to their parents, for only parents who care are worth fighting over.

Sibling rivalry diminishes in time—at least open warfare does—with the child's growing sense of identity, with the feelings of optimism and self-confidence that are fostered in significant part through play. In the meantime, there are no general rules indicating to what extent parents should interfere in their children's fights. Young children should probably be separated if their behavior becomes physically dangerous and given something to play with in temporary isolation. The object is not to squelch the children's aggression or even anger so much as to offer them other outlets for their energy.

In general, aggressive play shouldn't be squelched. Rather, parents and nursery school teachers should try to channel the energies of the youngsters in their charge in such a way that the children don't feel hemmed in. Active play on slides and swings, running, climbing and jumping are good outlets for the drive to demonstrate power and strength.

When children's aggressive energies are diverted, there is less likelihood that their play will erupt into open hostility. Common sense tells us that children need outlets for their aggressive urges far more than adults do, for they have yet to develop reasonable control of their feelings and behavior.

AGGRESSION TURNED
INWARD

Squelching aggressive play rather than providing good

outlets for it presents another hazard, too. The child who is scolded for rough play, constantly warned against hurting someone or something, may tend to hurt himself instead, becoming accident-prone in play. He gets the message that hurting himself is safer or more permissible to the adults in charge than venting his aggression on, say, his playthings. The child who is repeatedly cautioned against hurting others is bound to feel picked on—and consequently angry and guilty, too. With no approved outlets for his aggression, he lets out his energy and his anger on himself. Hurting himself serves two functions; it gives him an outlet for his strong feelings and also, because he is punishing himself, it relieves his feelings of guilt.

In general, we adults feel more comfortable when boys are aggressive and ready for rough competition than when girls play aggressively. We often speak of aggressive and openly competitive girls as being masculine in manner. Although it isn't certain whether our attitude reflects a biological or cultural difference between the sexes, it is true that in most cultures boys have always been more likely than girls to engage in aggressive play—in fistfights, wrestling and other combative behavior. However, this seems to be changing somewhat in recent years; our observations of girls in schools and on the streets and playgrounds lead us to believe that more girls these days fight like boys than used to be the case.

CONSTRUCTIVE OUTLETS

Whether or not girls are by nature as aggressive as boys, aggression is a component of virtually all play engaged in by both sexes from the earliest years. Indeed, play of various kinds provides one of the most constructive outlets there is for aggression. It is a safety valve for letting off steam that would very likely otherwise be expressed in dangerous ways—in hostility toward others or oneself, as we have seen.

Different kinds of aggressive play are more or less attractive to different people, of course, depending on individual physical and psychological makeup and a multitude of chance factors, as well.

Athletic contests and body contact sports that permit fighting within an amicable structure are particularly attractive to many people from early childhood on. Because these are games or sports, such contests are likely to be less humiliating to the loser than real fighting in anger would be. They are also likely to be safer for both the loser (the games have limits, which are usually adhered to) and for the winner, as well, who is not as likely to be subject to a knife-in-the-back retaliation as he would be if the fight had been real.

Not just body sports but virtually all games, including many we might not think of as aggressive, are actually "built" on aggression. The game of chess illustrates, perhaps more dramatically than any other, how games express aggression (including, sometimes, real hostility) and how they safely dispel such feelings. Chess might seem to be a peaceful game because it is a game of the intellect; it is sedentary and it is quiet. Indeed, the players often sit virtually motionlessly and hardly speaking for hours.

Actually, chess is one of the most aggressive of games. Beyond the fact that the game symbolizes war and is won by the conquest—the paralysis or death—of one army's king by the forces of the other army, the mental energy needed to play the game is tremendous. So exclusively focused on the game is the player's energy that, typically, he is unreachable while playing. Talk to him and he simply doesn't hear you, let alone answer. Moreover, many chess players freely admit to feeling considerable hostility toward their opponents while they are playing; while they are playing, the game of war is real to them.

Surely the highest expression of aggressive play is artistic activity. That all art is play, or the ideal fusion of work and play in which the two have become indistinguishable from each other, we think is self-evident. And all creative and artistic endeavors require plenty of aggressive energy, whether engaged in by children or adults. To "play" a musical instrument, even fairly competently, obviously requires great drive and persistence, as does achieving competence in any creative activity. Aggression is the fuel that powers the will to learn.

SEX PLAY

Many adults are even more distressed by child's play that has sexual overtones than they are by aggressive games.

Yet a fair amount of play does have a sexual component; this is especially apparent during the preschool and early school years, when children are eager to satisfy their curiosity about their bodies—the source of early sex-related child's play. By the age of eight or so, boys and girls have usually become rather circumspect and modest in matters pertaining to sex and are unlikely to play the kind of giggly, exploratory sex games characteristic of younger children.

As we have seen, children are extraordinarily curious from

birth—driven by nature to explore as much of themselves and their universe as their rapidly developing minds and senses will permit. Everything they can feel and touch, see and hear, excites their exploratory drive, including their own bodies—all parts of their bodies.

DISCOVERING THE
SEXUAL ORGANS

As mouths, fingers and toes are discovered and explored right from the beginning of life, so, fairly soon, is the baby's genital area, a naturally sensitive part of the body. This random exploration is the very earliest kind of sex-connected play. And it may be stimulated—in an altogether natural way—by the good feelings a baby has when his mother nurses him, when she holds him reassuringly and gently pats him dry after bathing and changing him. These early agreeable bodily experiences help to prepare the baby to enjoy caresses later in life. And, as well, they are a kind of early, preverbal sex education—the best kind, which relates sex to love, trust and dependability.

By the toddling stage, the child is well aquainted with all parts of his or her body and is likely to have an especially lively interest in the parts that are usually covered up— especially on other people. The young child now identifies himself or herself as a person, separate from all others but sharing the same basic equipment. And the child is anxious to compare himself with everyone else, to increase his understanding of what people are and how he fits into the human scheme of things.

The toddler is fascinated by the fact that he has a nose

just like Mommy's, and Mommy has eyebrows like his, hair and fingers, too. Toddlers also discover that some parts of their bodies are different from those of grown-ups. This excites their curiosity and their apprehension, too, particularly if the parent acts anxious about the child's discovery of his genitals and nervously removes the youngster's hand or even slaps it, if he or she touches that part of the body.

HOW MASTURBATION BEGINS

The sensitivity of the sexual areas of the body doesn't develop all at once in puberty; it already exists in infancy, perhaps at birth. All young children soon discover the capacity of this part of the body to produce pleasurable feelings when stimulated, and all at one time or another masturbate, manually or by squirming or rubbing their legs together.

Much as a young child may idly suck his thumb or fingers, so one can observe toddlers and preschoolers soothing and distracting themselves by masturbating. Young children frequently masturbate when they feel tense, worried or frightened.

Arlene Uslander, Caroline Weiss and Judith Telman, specialists in early education and authors of *Sex Education for Today's Child*, report that they have observed a considerable amount of masturbatory activity—especially among the boys in their classrooms—just before a scheduled test or pupil performance. And they note that the activity ceases as soon as the stressful situation has passed.

Masturbation should not be of great concern to adults

unless it is prolonged and frequent, and done in preference to, or in place of, all of the other wide-ranging exploratory activities of a child. As long as the child seems to be lively, active and generally flourishing, parents and teachers shouldn't infer that occasional masturbatory activities mean that something is wrong with the child.

To be sure, excessive masturbation is likely to be a sign that the child is troubled. It is not "bad" in itself, but it may indicate that the child isn't comfortable in his world and has chosen this way to make himself feel better. The parents of a young child who frequently masturbates, in public or private, shouldn't shame or frighten the child; but if the activity shows no signs of abating, they may wish to seek psychological counseling to discover and satisfy the youngster's underlying needs.

DOCTOR GAMES

Probably all preschoolers play "Doctor", the time-honored sex game with its various scenarios—getting a physical examination, going to the hospital to have a baby, giving an enema. Not surprisingly, young children often include the anal area in their sex games; after all, it is close to the genitals, also concealed by clothing, and unfortunately also thought of as "dirty".

Doctor games provide a made-to-order situation in which young children at play, especially youngsters of opposite sexes, can undress each other (it's only natural to get undressed in the doctor's office) and get a chance to see for themselves those mysterious differences between boys and girls.

We all remember playing Doctor from our own child-hoods. The universality of this game shows how important it is for young children who are just developing a sense of identity and self-assurance to satisfy their curiosity about how they're made, how they are like or unlike others. They want to be sure they're really OK and that there's nothing wrong with them.

Parents who come upon their preschoolers examining or "operating" on each other with lots of nervous giggling would do best to keep their own sense of humor and not to respond angrily, blowing the event all out of proportion. For one thing, the children probably already feel quite guilty about what they're up to, knowing full well that they're violating an adult taboo. Shaming them can only reinforce their suspicion that the private parts of their bodies aren't nice, and perhaps unclean, and that they, in their interest in their bodies, are bad.

DAYDREAMS AND FANTASY

Adults tend to worry that children with imaginary friends or those who engage in a great deal of fantasy-play will grow up to be liars—unable to tell the difference between fact and fiction, or simply indifferent to the truth. Actually, children who share all of their activities from breakfast to bedtime with an imaginary friend know full well that the imaginary friend really isn't there however much they may succeed in spoofing their parents.

As for knowing the difference between telling the truth or lying (say, about whether or not you put your toys away)—

and caring about it—this kind of conscience or fidelity to truth develops only gradually and is not something about which an adult can reasonably expect a preschool child to have a thorough understanding. In addition, as we tried to show earlier, fantasy-play—such as having an imaginary playmate, or spinning tall tales—is one of the most creative and intellectually stimulating forms of play there is.

Spinning fantasies, provided this isn't the child's only and continuous style of play, provides a needed retreat from the pressures of coping with the demands and intrusions of other people. It provides time to evaluate, make order and sense of all the impressions, the stimuli, which come at the child. In letting his imagination just "take off," the child is learning to think creatively. Such early fantasy-play provides a direct link to adult creativity. In speaking of his most creative years, Albert Einstein tells us, "When I examine myself and my methods of thought, I come to the conclusion that the gift of fantasy has meant more to me than my talent for abstract, positive thinking."

CHAPTER

V

Television Versus Play: The Dangerous Intruder

LITTLE more than thirty years old, television has profoundly changed the way we think and live and raise our children. It has changed the very world we live in—more, perhaps, than any other invention of the modern world, and in ways we never anticipated. Only during the last ten years have we begun to discover the effects of TV on young children.

On the average, children between the ages of two and five watch TV over thirty hours a week; a substantial number, measured in millions, are glued to the set for sixty or more hours a week. No other activity so dominates the lives of young children. Children between six and eleven watch a little less, about twenty to twenty-five hours a week on the average. Teenagers watch somewhat less than that.

In 1972, the Surgeon-General's study on TV and violence reported, essentially, that watching television can be dangerous to a child's health. Though we share that feeling, we think misleading application has been made of the Surgeon-General's study, which has been used to support the claim that there is a direct cause-and-effect relationship between violence seen on television and real violence in children and teenagers. Although programs with gratuitous violence—violence without a justifying or redeeming cause—are ugly, immoral and vicious, the incidence of violence in young children cannot be truly ascribed to watching violent programs.

EVALUATING TV VIOLENCE

Among the authorities most frequently quoted to support the presumed causal relationship between TV violence and violence in children is psychologist Albert Bandura of Stanford University, who has published numerous articles based on experiments he directed to investigate the degree to which children are likely to imitate the hostile and aggressive behavior as seen of adults on TV. As a result of his research, Dr. Bandura has concluded that there is little doubt that children imitate the violent acts they see in the movies and on television.

How reliable is this research?

In one of Dr. Bandura's studies, a small group of nursery school children were shown a simulated TV show in which an adult viciously attacked a large doll in a "novel" way—a way that children normally don't treat their playthings. The adult kicked the doll, threw it around, pounded it with a wooden hammer, all the while shouting such thing as "Pow" and "Socko." After seeing the show, the children—who were provided with dolls and hammers like those shown on the program—began to play in exactly the same manner as the aggressive adult they saw on the screen.

That the children who were exposed to this sham violence copied it doesn't seem to us to prove anything. Surely the children recognized that this astonishing adult behavior was an unusual kind of game. They must have wondered, indeed, what the grown-up was up to and why. In real life they had never seen an adult handle a doll in this way. In any case, even four-year-old children already well know that kicking, hitting and punching a doll and doing the same thing to a living creature are totally different actions. They must have known that such violence, however bizarre, wasn't nearly as wrong as harming a live person or animal would be.

Studies by other psychologists have come to different conclusions from those reached by Dr. Bandura. In their book, *Television and Aggression: An Experimental Field,* Drs. Seymour Feshbach and Robert D. Singer describe a study with a group of boys selected at random. One group was exposed to television programs showing violent acts; the other group, serving as a control, were shown programs of a peaceful nature. The researchers also observed the boys in both groups to determine their natural methods of play. The results of the experiment showed that the boys who were not prone to fighting in their everyday lives did not act aggressively after watching violent behavior on television. On the other hand, the boys who were already given to fighting and rough behavior did act up after they watched both the peaceful and the violent programs. Evidently these boys got "turned on" to aggression by television, whatever the nature of the show.

A further finding was that the boys who engaged in little fantasy play in their everyday lives—who did not act out their anger in fantasies—were the most prone to act aggressively after watching television. Included in the benefits of fantasy play, as we noted earlier, is a decrease in hostile aggression among those children who work it out in fantasy.

Another study, conducted by psychologists Stanley Milgram and Lance R. Shotland, also casts doubt on the claim that there is a direct cause-and-effect relationship between fictionalized violence and antisocial behavior in children. To test the hypothesis that antisocial actions seen on TV induce imitation in children, the researchers created a "stimulus" TV program, depicting the acts of breaking into and stealing from a bank. The program was shown to a group of young children who were then taken to a gift distribution center where they could imitate the kind of antisocial behavior they had seen. The results were ambiguous: the program provoked some imitative behavior but to such a minor degree that it wasn't considered statistically significant. The researchers then developed three other "stimulus" programs and set up testing situations specifically designed to make it easy for the children to copy the antisocial behavior. These three TV programs "produced no evidence of imitation."

In all of the controversy over TV violence and real violence in children, only the studies allegedly proving such a connection are widely quoted. Those which fail to show a connection between TV violence and real violence are, for the most part, unpublicized and disregarded.

It seems to us that blaming one aspect of television—violent programming—for real violence allows us to ignore the danger to preschoolers of television itself and, as well, permits us to avoid facing the fact that violence has its real roots in complex familial and social conditions. What may make children violent are the brutalizing effects of poverty and abuse. It is the children already endangered by the circumstances of their lives—those who are already prone to violence—who are further encouraged in this tendency by the very act of watching television.

THE REAL HAZARDS
OF TELEVISION

We believe that TV viewing is hazardous to a young child's development, but not only, or mainly, because of the quality of the programs they watch. The oft-repeated truism, "It's not the quantity, but the quality that counts," which is usually said about the amount of time parents spend with their children, could be turned around in speaking of the time young children spend with their TV sets. It is not the quality but the quantity that counts. The more, the worse. Of course, good TV shows are much better for children than poor ones; but whether the shows are good or bad, prolonged TV-watching imperils young children.

As kittens naturally spend most of their first months playing—that is, practicing to be cats—so children naturally spend most of their first years playing—that is, practicing to be mature human beings. The worst thing about TV is that it replaces essential play activities with nothing, with passivity rather than activity.

To grasp the essence of why regular, heavy TV viewing is so hazardous to young children—even retarding the development of a child's sense of identity, his sense of himself as a person like others—it's necessary to consider the effect of activity, or the lack of it, on a child's overall development.

ALL TRUE PLAY
IS ACTIVE

What precisely is the function of activity in the child's earliest years? How does play, above all, fulfill this function? Why does heavy TV viewing, above all, inhibit it? What do we mean when we say that watching television is essentially passive—how, that is, does it differ from sitting still and listening to a story?

As we have tried to show throughout this book, young children learn almost everything they need to know through the powers of play—how to get along in the world; how to solve intellectual, social and emotional problems; how to cope with stress and heal themselves of hurt.

Why does play work to fulfill these goals? It works because it is spontaneous, self-teaching exercise. True play is always active and full of effort. We do not exclude quiet play, such as daydreaming, from this definition for daydreaming is an activity of the mind, often an intense and very concentrated one.

A half-century ago, Jean Piaget published his first pioneering studies of how children learn. As his extensive observations showed, young children learn through self-motivated, discovery play, inventing both the problems and their solutions to them according to an innate and universal "readiness" timetable. True, the timetable for learning is subject to individual variations, but the vehicle—discovery play—that leads to the stages of learning is the same for all children.

Subsequent studies by Piaget and other students of child development have substantiated and reinforced these findings. Lasting learning follows from the discoveries children make for themselves through play. Children make intellectual discoveries (such as the fact that water runs out of a cup with a hole in it), social and emotional discoveries (how to win friends and influence parents), physical discoveries (how to climb a stepladder and get down again safely).

One can say, in a sense, that the child's urge to learn by doing is our human "program". As lower animals are "programmed" to survive by instinct, we are "programmed" to survive by discoveries made through trial and error.

Self-directed practice-play is how a young child carries out the human program for survival. When a child repeats a just-learned word or phrase over and over for his own ears only and with every sign of delight, the parent recognizes that the child is beginning to teach himself to talk. He is playing in the way that suits his needs best at the moment.

TV UNDERCUTS
ACTIVE PLAY

Television can do nothing to invite the child to discover, to learn on his own. First, of course, it robs the child of the hours needed for play. Worse, it tends to hypnotize the child, to blank out his connections with himself and the world. It deprives him of the opportunity to respond actively to an incoming stimulus, subjecting him instead to a bombardment of sound and pictures at a pace he cannot control or alter. Whether the program is "educational" and designed for young children or not, it prevents the child from exercising his own mind and imagination.

In being read to or told a story, a child has to make up his own images about the people, events, scenes in the story. He brings them to life in his imagination. Moreover, he has considerable control over the pace and rhythm of the material presented. Children often ask an adult who is reading to them to go back and read something over, or to stop and talk about what is happening on the page. None of this is possible in watching television. The story rushes on, the prefabricated images flash on and off.

THE FLAWS IN
EDUCATIONAL TV

Some of the "educational" programs for preschoolers which are designed to teach reading and math skills seem to us even more likely to be harmful for young children than many "conventional" programs. First, as we have shown, it is undesirable to impose adult-structured game-lessons on preschoolers. In addition, such shows frequently present the material to be learned at a frantic pace. We have seen segments of *Sesame Street*, for example, designed to teach spelling rules or an understanding of abstract concepts such as "round", which consist of a barrage of brilliantly colored images zooming on and off the screen to the accompaniment of loud rock music. The editing is stylishly rapid; the effect is modern, attractive, sophisticated. The skill it takes to put such a presentation together is enormous. But is it good for young children? We don't think so. Such a rat-a-tat bombardment of children's senses allows them no opportunity to respond with their own feelings or thoughts.

The impact on a young child can be devastating. The child is just beginning to be able to conceptualize and to understand and control his feelings and behavior. He needs time and freedom to practice thinking and ways of behaving on his own.

For older children the perils of television are less grave. For one thing, they usually watch it less than preschoolers do. For another, they have already presumably acquired the foundation for higher levels of learning during the first five years or so of life. Presumably. It seems to us that heavy TV-viewing in the early years is surely one of the prime causes for the sorry performance in schools during the past decade and more.

OVERCOMING
THE TV MENACE

There are two broad approaches to overcoming the menace of TV for preschoolers—short, that is, of throwing out the set, a step which some families have taken but which most are simply not going to consider. First, however exhausting it may be to set limits on TV watching and to make the rules stick, it's worth the effort. How much TV should be permitted? Every family must decide for itself. We recommend no more than an hour a day; less is better, except for special family programs broadcast in the evening, from time to time, which the children may be allowed to watch and then encouraged to talk about with each other and their parents.

The TV habit, like all bad habits, is more easily prevented than cured. In homes where it never got started, parents report no problems in setting limits. At the other extreme, where parents are hard pressed to limit viewing time, some solve the problem by disconnecting the set, either by removing the cord altogether (if it's the kind that plugs into both the wall and the set), or simply by unplugging the cord and closing the wall outlet with a special plug.

In addition to limiting viewing time, it is most important for adults to monitor the shows watched. Parents should not permit young children to watch shows they think are too frantic, too violent, too dumb or distasteful.

When a show has been approved, parents should watch along with the child, at least some of the time, so that afterwards they can talk to the children about what happened on the show. Who did the youngsters like best? Why? Was there someone or something they didn't like? Why? If it was a skit or story, parents might ask the children if they think such a story could really take place, or what else might have happened. The aim is to try to elicit a thoughtful response to the show on the part of the child. If the program was one of the better nursery-format ones like *Mister Rogers' Neighborhood* or *Romper Room* and showed live children and adults, the parents might do some of the activities shown on the program with their children at home.

As co-directors of the Yale University Family Television Research and Consultation Center, psychologists Dorothy and Jerome Singer have conducted extensive studies on children and television. They have observed that when adults approach children who are watching television and begin to play an interesting game, the children often join the game, drifting away—and staying away—from the set, even after the adults leave. The Singers suggest encouraging children to make up games and skits based on television programs, and to put on their own shows—constructing the TV set out of a carton, and using dolls or cardboard cutout figures as puppet players.

Sharing children's television viewing and using it to initiate active play involves more adult direction in children's play than may be ideal—ideal, that is, if the children were playing in the first place. The adult's main role is to be a member of the audience, not the director of the show. It may take considerable effort to wean young children who have already formed the TV habit away from the set, but it's well worth the effort. The reward? Very likely, a more eager learner. Almost certainly, a healthier and happier child.

TV AND SOCIETY:
THE DANGEROUS CONNECTION

The destructive impact of television on young children which is, in itself, considerable is even greater than it might be if the world we lived in were different. But, as we said at the beginning of this book, our mobile and rapidly changing society already deprives children of useful knowlege about the world of adults and, therefore, of the "raw material" for the "let's pretend" play that is vital to the development of competence and a feeling of belonging to the world.

A heavy diet of television can only make matters worse. This applies to all children, and for some it may even be the last straw. As we have seen, though one cannot establish a direct cause-and-effect relationship between violence on TV and real violence in children, we have also seen that television is an exacerbating factor in the lives of young children who are already prone to violence.

Who are these children, and why does watching television increase their propensity for violence? They are children who, in one sense or another, have suffered abuse or neglect in their early lives. They are most likely to have grown up in extreme and frustrating poverty. And extreme poverty today is likely to be much harder to bear than it was in the past. It is harder to submit to because our society has promised so much and delivered so little to its marginal people—to the inherited poor, the uneducated, the non-whites. Our society has raised their expectations, then shattered their hopes, again and again. The frustration, born of repeatedly broken promises, is more damaging to the human spirit than is hardship itself.

What must be the impact of television on young children brought up in deep poverty? Virtually every family, even in the poorest of homes, has a television set. Moreover, the children in these homes, frequently lacking the presence of a caring adult or perhaps of any adult, are especially likely to be glued to the set all day. What they see there is even more insulting to their spirit, more damaging to their minds, than TV fare is to children living in more privileged circumstances.

The tantalizing stories of a world of power and riches; the commercials showing beautiful people using luxurious products; the sentimental skits about families living in clean and tidy homes and wrapping up their problems every half hour; the terrifying scenes of violence and brutality—how must these affect children already impoverished in their opportunities for creative, mind-opening play? To grow up whole in so dehumanizing an environment seems to us miraculous. That many children achieve this miracle is testimony to the flexibility of the human mind and spirit, testimony to the children's strength and grace under pressure. But many do not make it.

Imagine the confusion, frustration, rage that gradually builds up in many of these youngsters as they realize that they have scarcely any hope of entering the successful, free-spending "establishment" pictured on television. And they learn this early. For in spite of what we like to believe about our country, the gap between rich and poor, particularly between white and minorities—as measured by unemployment rates and total wages—is not decreasing. Indeed, for teenagers it is increasing.

Moreover, it is especially difficult for the parents of children in such homes to transmit their own standards and values to their children, for among the things the children learn on television is that what counts the most in our society is securing money, status and success. Because these children soon discover that their parents are poor and are victims of society, they don't find them believable or worthy of respect.

There is a new kind of anarchic behavior, a new kind of crime, frighteningly widespread in our cities and suburbs today—the "senseless" crime committed by children and teenagers from such backgrounds. These are crimes that are committed for no reason at all. We are not speaking of muggings for money but assaults for the sake of assault. This kind of behavior seems impossible to comprehend unless one assumes that the young people who commit such acts don't feel they have anything in common with their victims; unless one assumes they have failed to develop a basic sense of identity as humans like others.

In *Criminal Violence, Criminal Justice*, Charles E. Silberman discussing this kind of senseless crime, writes about three boys, twelve and thirteen years old, who first set fire to a cat and then murdered a sleeping derelict by dousing him with lighter fluid and setting him on fire. The author notes that the boys' "absence of affect is the most frightening aspect of all. In the past, juveniles who exploded into violence tended to feel considerable guilt or remorse afterward; the new criminals have been so brutalized in their upbringing that they seem incapable of viewing their victims as fellow human beings, or of realizing that they have killed another person."

Poverty and oppression have always been with us—actually, more terribly in earlier times than now. Yet crimes like these have become common only recently. Poverty has always bred violence and lawlessness but not in the past "motiveless" crime. What is different now? It is the mounting frustration and rage born of shattered hope among the outcasts of our society. And it is television. It is the cumulative effect of having been saturated during early childhood—the crucial years for development—with a daily diet of television.

It is beyond the scope of this book to explore the remedies for the social inequities that breed violence. What we can do is suggest that as citizens we support those measures that can at least partially counteract some of the destructive conditions of society. There may be no social need of greater importance, no measure of greater potential benefit, than the provision of free or low-cost, high-quality nursery services for families who cannot provide their young children with protective and stimulating care. There is no nation in the Western world that does not far surpass the United States in the quantity and quality of government-funded day-care programs. By actively supporting the long-delayed passage of adequate day-care legislation, we can give millions of children the chance to play and learn, the chance to grow up able to function successfully in the world. We may even help to save our society from mounting violence and anarchic crime.

RESTORING THE
WORLD OF PLAY

Most of the children in our country live much more privileged lives than do the very poor, and are not as vulnerable to the destructive impact of television. Even so, these children—middle-class children—are also threatened, sometimes gravely, by the aspects of our uprooted, technological society which deprive them, as we have seen, of the subject matter for their let's-pretend games.

In his provocative essay, "Play and the Uses of Immaturity," Jerome Bruner discusses a widespread phenomenon of our time—the middle-class, antisocial "drop-out" adolescent. He hypothesizes that such behavior is itself a distorted kind of play. Bruner suggests that the adolescents who play these dangerous games (which really echo the games preschoolers play in that they, too, involve "discovering" who they are and seeking way of coping with the stresses of the world) do so because they were deprived in early childhood of opportunities for imaginative, individual and social play.

The drug use, the running away, the panhandling, drifting and grifting—all the anti-establishment behavior so widespread among middle-class children today stems from their ignorance of their own abilities, from a feeling of alienation from society and an urgent need to find out what they and the world are like. Unfortunately, however, these games of adolescence are acted out, and dangerously so, in the real world. This kind of risky "play" might well have been forestalled if the teenagers had had the chance to forge connections to society, to explore their feelings, play their make-believe games at the natural time, in the natural way.

What then can be done to restore to young children opportunities for spontaneous, imaginative play? There is a great deal we can do to affect public policy and our private lives, as well. We were speaking about the need for day-care services to Dr. Eward Zigler, the first director of the U.S. Office of Child Development, now Stirling Professor of Psychology at Yale. Dr. Zigler observed that proposals for day-care bills have been developed then dropped by Congress, session after session, not only because of public apathy and opposition from the White House but also because of disagreement among the experts about setting standards. As Dr. Zigler pointed out, "The endless dispute over the fine points in legislation unhappily results in no legislation. Even the passage of a less-than-perfect bill would be a tremendous step forward."

Those who believe that "day-care legislation is absolutely essential now," as the drafters of the 1980 proposal for a national child-care bill state, can support such legislation by writing to their congressmen about this issue. Those who want to know more, not only about day care but also about a wide variety of issues of concern to parents and children, can write to the Coalition for Children and Youth, a national nonprofit association (815 15th Street, N.W., Washington, D.C. 20005), and an excellent source of information about issues, conferences and programs pertaining to the family.

In addition to supporting legislation for affordable day care for all families who need such services, some parents may be interested in starting co-op centers of their own. (See the Bibliography under Belle E. Evans, et. al. for a comprehensive guide to starting a co-op center or play school, small or large.)

There is, as well, a great deal we can do in our everyday lives to restore the world of play to our children and make our cities and suburbs better and more inviting places for children to play in.

In a spirit of play and adventure, parents and teachers can take young children on visits and excursions to real work places, not just to museums, historical restorations, zoos and the like, but to great markets and factories, to fire-houses, carpentry and machine shops, textile mills, lumber yards. And, of course, we can bring them from time to time to the places where we ourselves work so they will know what we do and can act it out in their role-playing games.

We can join—or start—block or neighborhood associations to plant trees and flowers, clean up the streets, develop local recreational and health centers, hold arts and crafts fairs. By taking part in such activities—along with our children—we do more than improve the general look and atmosphere of our neighborhoods. We counter the impersonality of our society and help make it comprehensible and satisfying to our children—and ourselves, as well. And by so doing, we provide our children with the raw material for imaginative play and the desire to engage in it, which they need to grow up whole and sound.

In virtually every community today, there are several kinds of volunteer programs already underway—programs that satisfy people's needs to have control over their lives and to feel they belong to the place where they live, share common interests with their neighbors.

New York City alone has 10,000 block associations and community groups. The Alliance for Volunteerism estimates that there are six million voluntary associations in the United States working in various ways to restore a sense of community to people living in cities and suburbs across the country. This tremendous grass roots movement reflects the determination of the "common man" to regain the individual power and satisfaction our advanced technology has deprived us of. The National Association of Neighborhoods (1612 20th Street, N.W., Washington, D.C. 20009) can provide information about the kinds of projects that have been undertaken by community and neighborhood associations. Churches and temples are excellent sources of information on organizing neighborhood projects, and they frequently make their facilities available for community programs.

In depriving children of the time, space and opportunity to play spontaneously and imaginatively, safely and freely, we have really robbed them of their childhood. We cannot turn the clock back. But we can, as parents and teachers in our homes and nursery schools, and as members of our communities working together, restore to the young children now growing up their right and their ability to play for their lives.

Bibliography

Almy, Millie (Ed.). *Early Childhood Play: Selected Readings Related to Cognition and Motivation.* New York: Selected Academic Readings, 1968.

Auerbach, Stevanne. *Confronting the Child Care Crisis.* Boston: Beacon Press, 1979.

Biber, Barbara. *Play As a Growth Process.* Pamphlet. New York: Bank Street Publications.

_____. *Promoting Cognitive Growth in Children.* Washington, D.C.: National Association for the Education of Young Children, 1971.

Bremer, Anne, and Bremmer, John. *Open Education: A Beginning.* New York: Holt, Rinehart & Winston, 1972.

Bruner, Jerome. *The Process of Education.* Cambridge: Harvard University Press, 1965.

————; Jolly, Alison; Sylva, Kathy (Eds.). *Play—Its Role in Development and Evolution.* New York: Basic Books, 1976.

Caplan, Frank, and Caplan, Theresa. *The Power of Play.* New York: Doubleday & Co., 1973.

Carmichael, Carrie. *Non-Sexist Childraising.* Boston: Beacon Press, 1977.

Cohen, Dorothy, and Rudolph, Marguerita. *Kindergarten and Early Schooling.* Englewood Cliffs, N.J.: Prentice-Hall, 1977.

Erikson, Erik. *Childhood and Society.* New York: W.W. Norton & Co., 1964.

Evans, Belle E.; Shub, Beth; and Weinstein, Marlene. *Day Care: How to Plan, Develop and Operate a Day Care Center.* Boston: Beacon Press, 1971.

Gessell, Arnold; Ilg, Frances L.; Ames, Louise Bates; and Rodell, Janet Learned. *Infant and Child in the Culture of Today*, rev. ed. New York: Harper & Row, 1974.

Glickman, Beatrice Marden, and Springer, Nesha Bass. *Who Cares for the Baby? Choices in Child Care.* New York: Schocken Books, 1978.

Gordon, Ira J.; Guinach, Barry; and Jester, J. Emile. *Child Learning Through Child Play.* New York: St. Martin's Press, 1972.

Herron, Robin, and Sutton-Smith, Brian. *Child's Play.* New York: John Wiley & Sons, 1971.

Hirsch, Elizabeth. *The Block Book.* Washington, D.C.: National Association for the Education of Young Children, 1974.

Koste, Virginia Glasgow. *Dramatic Play in Childhood: Rehearsal for Life.* New Orleans: Anchorage Press, 1978.

Marzullo, Jean, and Lloyd, Janice. *Learning Through Play.* New York: Harper & Row, 1972.

Millar, Susanna. *The Psychology of Play.* New York: Penguin Books, 1968.

Piaget, Jean. *Play, Dreams and Imitation.* New York: W.W. Norton & Co., 1962.

Piers, Maria W. *Growing Up With Children.* New York: Quadrangle/The New York Times Co., 1966.

———, (Ed.). *Play and Development.* New York: W.W. Norton & Co., 1972.

Sharp, E. *Thinking is Child's Play.* New York: Avon Books, 1969.

Silberman, Charles E. *Criminal Violence, Criminal Justice.* New York: Random House, 1978.

Singer, Jerome L. *The Child's World of Make-Believe.* New York: Academic Press, 1973.

———, and Singer, Dorothy G. *Partners in Play: A Step-by-Step Guide to Imaginative Play in Children.* New York: Harper & Row, 1977.

Smart, Mollie S., and Smart, Russell C. *Children: Deve-*

lopment and Relationships. New York: Macmillan Publishing Co., 1967.

Sparling, Joseph, and Lewis, Isabelle. *Learningames for the First Three Years: A Guide to Parent-Child Play*. New York: Walker and Company, 1979.

Sponseller, Doris. *Play As a Learning Medium*. Washington, D.C.: National Association for the Education of Young Children, 1974.

Uslander, Arlene S.: Weiss, Caroline; and Telman, Judith. *Sex Education for Today's Child*. New York: Association Press, 1977.

Zigler, Edward. *Headstart: The Legacy of America's War on Poverty*. New York: Free Press, 1979.

Play for the Handicapped

A Reader's Guide for Parents of Children with Mental, Physical or Emotional Disabilities. Rockville, Md.: U.S. Department of Health, Education, and Welfare, Bureau of Community Health Services, 1976.

Caldwell, Bettye M., and Stedman, Donald J. (Eds.). *Infant Education: A Guide for Helping Handicapped Children in the First Three Years*. New York: Walker and Company, 1977.

Let's-Play-to-Grow (12-packet activity kit for the handicapped). Available from the Joseph P. Kennedy, Jr. Foundation, 1701 K Street, N.W., Washington, D.C. 20006.

White, Robin. *The Special Child*. Boston: Little, Brown & Co., 1978.

Index